HOW TO SURVIVE ᴵᴺ A DEAD CHURCH

And other congregational hazards to your spiritual health.

Doug Batchelor with Karen Lifshay

HOW TO SURVIVE IN A DEAD CHURCH

And other congregational hazards to your spiritual health.

Doug Batchelor with Karen Lifshay

Pacific Press Publishing Association
Boise, Idaho
Oshawa, Ontario, Canada

Edited by Jerry D. Thomas
Designed by Dennis Ferree
Cover and inside art by Bruce Day
Typeset in 11/13 Garamond

Unless otherwise indicated, all scriptural references in this
book are from the New King James Version.

Library of Congress Cataloging-in-Publication Data:
Batchelor, Doug, 1957-
    How to survive in a dead church : and other congregational
hazards to your spiritual health / Doug Batchelor with Karen
Lifshay.
        p.   cm.
    ISBN 0-8163-1197-8
    1. Christian life— Seventh-day Adventist authors. 2. Church
renewal—Seventh-day Adventists. 3. Seventh-day Adventists—
Membership. 4. Adventists—Membership. 5. Sabbatarians—
Membership. I. Lifshay, Karen, 1959-   . II. Title.
BV4501.2.B384193   1994
248.4'867—dc20   93-35906
                                                      CIP

94 95 96 97 98 ● 5 4 3 2 1

Dedication

This book is dedicated to:

. . . the many Christian soldiers who lie wounded and alone on the battlefield of life.
HOLD ON; A MEDIC IS COMING.

. . . all the AWOL troops wandering in a foreign land.
IT'S TIME TO REENLIST.

. . . and to our Commander-in-Chief, Jesus Christ.
HE IS THE GREATEST SURVIVOR OF ALL TIME!

"Upon this rock I will build my church; and the gates of hell shall not prevail against it" (Matthew 16:18).

Special Thanks

It was Andrew Carnegie who had the following profound words inscribed on his tombstone:

"Here lies a man that was smart enough to surround himself with smarter men."

I'm not saying that I am so smart; however, this book is an example of how that principle works. I have tried to surround myself with talented friends and family in the hope that it would be contagious.

I would like to begin by thanking my partner—my wife, Karen, for her practical advice and patience as this book was being written while she enjoyed ten months of pregnancy (it was a boy, eight pounds, seven ounces). Also her mother, Bonnie, for the hours of typing and arranging material. I'm indebted to more friends than I can name who shared with me their perspectives, observations, and suggestions in areas where we need to "survive."

I want to also give special recognition to Karen Lifshay. When this project began to drift into the vacuum of unfinished books, her material on "surviving singles" and "surviving disappointments" helped to enrich this book as well as to replace missing teeth in other sections. Were it not for her many hours of creative contributions and art concepts, this book would probably still be in my "to do" file!

Thanks to all.

Gratefully,
Doug Batchelor

Contents

Introduction

An epidemic! That's the only term I can think of to describe the plague of wounded feelings, confusion, indifference, and just plain lack of commitment that is causing a frightening fallout among Seventh-day Adventist Church members.

In the last twelve years, I have worked as a pastor and an evangelist—mostly as an evangelist. As I travel from one church to another preparing for a campaign, I encourage church members to invite their friends, as well as inactive and former members, to come to the meetings.

As I visit with people who are attending the meetings, I usually find some former church members. During the visit, I will politely ask, "Friend, why did you stop coming to church?"

Generally I will hear one of the following answers:

"Somebody done me wrong." This song usually heads the list. "Somebody, or some group in the church, hurt my feelings, and I don't ever want to see them again. That's why I don't go to church anymore. Those hypocrites!"

The biggest problem with churches is that there are people in them. If we could just get all the people out of the church, there wouldn't be nearly as many problems!

"The church seems dead. The services are painfully boring, and I don't get anything out of them." As though we only go to church to see what we can get or to be entertained.

"I'm not good enough to go to church." This sounds like someone saying, "I'm too sick to go to the hospital."

"I've just been too busy lately, so much work to do." That's the purpose for the Sabbath. Are we too busy for God?

"I'm not sure I believe these things anymore." No wonder! If you spent a little more time on your knees with the

Bible and less time on your couch with the remote control, you might believe differently.

"I'm so tired every Sabbath." We are rarely too tired to go to some sports event or shopping. People generally do what they want to do.

"The church is too far from our house." If Jesus was willing to travel a million light-years from heaven to earth to save us, we can probably find a way to get to His house once a week to thank Him.

Forgive me if I sound a little cynical, but I can't help wondering what the angels must think of our indifference toward the privilege of worshiping our Lord and Saviour.

Remember the parable Jesus told of a king who invited many guests to a great marriage supper for his son? When the time came to attend the supper, all the guests, in one accord, began to make excuses (see Luke 14:16-20). It sometimes appears that the only thing the church can do in one accord is to make excuses.

Please remember, the Bible tells us that before God poured out the Holy Spirit on the early disciples, they were all in one place and in one accord.

For ten days before that marvelous event, the disciples had to pray and put away their petty differences. We read in the Bible that they, too, had their share of problems and differences (Luke 22:24).

I repeat: before the outpouring of God's Spirit, they were together in one place (Acts 2:1). I think that's significant, because a few days earlier, Jesus was betrayed, and the disciples scattered everywhere (Matthew 26:21, 56).

God gave His Spirit to His people only after they had come together spiritually in their relationships and physically under one roof.

Remember, Jesus said: "Where two or three come together in my name, there am I with them" (Matthew 18:20, NIV). There is a special blessing promised when we gather together in His name!

You might be wondering, Why do we need a book on how

to survive in church? The answer is very simple. In the book *The Acts of the Apostles,* page 12, Ellen G. White states, "Enfeebled and defective as it may appear, the church is the one object upon which God bestows in a special sense His supreme regard."

If the church is the object of God's supreme regard, then it stands to reason it would naturally be the object upon which the devil concentrates his most intense rage. The dragon was "wroth" with the woman (Revelation 12:17).

Now, here is the heart of this book. I believe Jesus is coming soon, very soon, maybe too soon for most. Before that great day, Jesus will once again pour out His Holy Spirit, in latter rain and Pentecostal power. But first, we must repeat the experience of the early disciples and be in one place and of one accord. That means to be able to worship together in Christian unity. Remember, Jesus' final prayer was for us to be one. The devil has come down with great wrath because he knows his time is short (see Revelation 12:12). I only wish we all knew it too!

Just as a wolf must scatter the lambs from the flock and from the shepherd before he can bring one down, the devil is working frantically to separate God's sheep from the Shepherd, the fold, and from one another, so he can claim his prey.

This book is dedicated to exposing some (not all) of the devil's most common traps and tricks used to catapult people out of church fellowship. It is with an earnest desire and prayer that, as the great final storm approaches, we might press closer to our Shepherd and to one another.

Keep the faith!
D.E.B.

Chapter 1

Why Join a Church?

Let us consider one another to provoke unto love and to good works: Not forsaking the assembling of ourselves together, as the manner of some is; but exhorting one another: and so much the more, as ye see the day approaching (Hebrews 10:24, 25, KJV).

You can be a Christian without joining a church if:

> **. . . you can be a bee without a hive.**

> **. . . you can be a soldier without an army.**

> **. . . you can be a salesperson without customers.**

> **. . . you can be a politician who is a hermit.**

> **. . . you can be a football player without a team.**

A man who was raised in Russia recently immigrated to the United States. He wanted to be a good American citizen, so he tried to conform to as many American customs as possible.

"What do Americans eat for breakfast?" he asked a friend one day.

"Well, most people eat cereal," said the friend.

So, our Russian immigrant headed for the nearest mega-supermarket and asked the clerk where he could find the cereal. The clerk directed him to an aisle longer than an airport terminal.

She told him, "Take your pick!"

Stacks and stacks of cereal of all descriptions and colors lined both sides of the aisle. Hot cereal, cold cereal, big boxes, little boxes, and children's cereal with cartoon characters on the front or athletes advertising prizes inside. Some cereal was almost pure sugar; some had no sugar. There was instant cereal and fiber flakes.

Our Russian friend wandered aimlessly up and down the aisle, not knowing how to choose a box of cereal or where to begin. He was dazed by the selection of just cereal!

Companies like Kellogg's make many different cereals that appeal to a broad spectrum of society. In that way, they hope to capture a large share of the consumer market.

Likewise, the devil has created a wide variety of false religions and objects of worship to capture a larger part of the world-worship market. Some people think the devil is against religion. Wrong! He is for it. From the time of the Garden of Eden, Satan has known that humankind was created with the desire to worship. He has tried to trap people by telling them it doesn't matter how a person worships, so long as that person is religious.

Cain fell for Satan's trap. He made an offering and then killed his brother, Abel. The men who crucified Jesus were extremely religious. Yes, the Bible tells us that even those who receive the mark of the beast in the last days will be worshiping.

Satan is not against religion, but he is against the truth of Christ's religion. That is why he tries to confuse people about whether or not they should join a church.

I took a survey to determine why people join a church, and here are some of the answers I received:

1. It's the church of my parents.
2. It's close to our home.
3. The people are friendly and loving.
4. The music is beautiful.
5. The preacher is handsome or dynamic.
6. It has a good children's program.

7. The building is impressive.
8. The important or influential people go to this church.
9. The services are exciting.
10. The church needs me.

Though each of these elements is good in and of itself, none—not one of them—is the right reason to join a church.

There is only one right reason to join a church—because the foundation teachings of that church, or denomination, are the teachings of the Bible and of Jesus; the pillars of that church are based on the truth of God, and you are committed to following truth.

Sadly, most people shop for a church the way children choose breakfast cereal. They like the picture on the box, or they want the prize inside, while missing the most important criteria—reading the ingredients.

The first and most important test to apply to any church is:

Are the teachings of this church (not of one or two individuals in this church but the official position of the movement) consistent with the teachings of Jesus?

If the teachings of that denomination are the teachings of Christ and the Bible, then that is God's church.

You should hang in there even if:

. . . the people are cantankerous and crabby.
. . . the singing sounds like feeding time at the zoo.
. . . the church building is a renovated hamburger stand.
. . . the pastor's sermons are so boring that even the bats leave the belfry at eleven o'clock every Sabbath morning.
. . . the members are so divided that there is a fluorescent line painted down the middle of the sanctuary.
. . . the people come to church driving army tanks.

Do you wonder if God's church really exists? Now, just suppose that God does have a church somewhere that holds the truth. Would it look like the "perfect" church? On the contrary, it would be the supreme object of Satan's rage and attract his concentrated attention. The devil would try to introduce as many problems and conflicts into the church as possible to discourage the members and newcomers. He would inspire the world to accuse them of being a cult. He would try to entice them to jump ship, to throw in the towel, or to stop fighting the fight of faith.

Now, I realize that church membership is not an elevator to heaven, and many—maybe even most—of those whose names are on a church membership roll here on earth may not be citizens of God's kingdom in heaven. At the same time, Satan knows that "united we stand, but divided we fall," so he is working with a frenzy to divide God's people and scatter the army until our power evaporates.

This is why it is so important that we glue our hands to the plow, squeeze until our knuckles are white, and never look back or let go (see Luke 9:62)!

If you really love Jesus and are committed to truth, you will want to be a part of His church. He wants you to join His family, faulty though it may be.

All this may leave you with the question: If I join, how can I survive? Just follow me through the following chapters and see.

Chapter 2

Surviving in a Dead Church

Because iniquity shall abound, the love of many shall wax cold (Matthew 24:12, KJV).

You know you are in a dead church when:

> . . . there are oxygen bottles at the end of every pew.

> . . . the people don't read the bulletin. They just use it to doodle on during the sermon.

> . . . the people sing the hymn "Stand up, stand up for Jesus" while still sitting down.

> . . . the members look like they've been baptized in lemon juice.

> . . . the only witnessing program during the year is Ingathering.

> . . . the youngest member of the church is on Social Security.

> . . . the members could be mistaken for mannequins Sabbath morning if they didn't snore.

I remember a true story about a school bus loaded with children that was caught in a terrible blizzard. The bus slid off the road into a ditch and became hopelessly stuck. The driver knew it might be hours before help would come down that isolated country road. So he left the engine running with the heat on to keep the children from freezing and went tramping off into the deep snow, looking for help.

Before leaving, he asked a responsible twelve-year-old named Tony to take charge until he returned. Soon after the bus driver left, the bus engine stopped. Tony tried desperately to start the motor again, but to no avail.

Quickly, the temperature dropped below freezing inside the bus, and the children began to shake and whimper. As time went by, some of the children began to drop off to sleep. Tony knew that if the children fell asleep, they'd freeze to death. So he went from one child to another, shaking them, shouting at them, and in some cases slapping them, working frantically to keep them awake and moving.

A few hours later, the driver returned with help, and the children were all safely rescued. Later, Tony was given a medal for heroism. Tony didn't feel he deserved to be called a hero. He said that in the process of keeping all the other children warm and awake, he knew he was also keeping himself warm and awake.

Friends, that's how it is in God's church. One of the best ways for you to experience a revival in a cold, sleepy, or dead church is to share Jesus with others. Keeping them awake will help keep you warm and awake!

Before you excuse yourself from reaching out to wake up the saints by saying you don't have enough experience, let me say that you have exactly the same qualifications the twelve apostles had when they started.

When the Lord first ordained the twelve apostles, He sent them out preaching, even though they were not completely converted. Sharing their faith was part of their conversion-training process.

So if you think you are in a cold church, get involved like Tony. You can gather warmth from the coldness of others. An igloo may be made of ice, but it keeps the Eskimos warm!

Here are some things you can do to survive in a cold or dead church:

1. Start a Bible-study group. Some people who don't come to church will feel more comfortable in a home Bible study. If you come to church already warm from studying during the week, you will have some heat to share.

2. Get some good spiritual audio- or videocassette tapes. Listen to these tapes, and then pass them around. Again, this is like giving a bowl of hot soup to someone shivering and hungry.

3. Make a boring or uninteresting Sabbath School class come alive. Ask some thought-provoking questions that stimulate discussion. For example, "How can I know if I'm really converted?" Or, "Can a person be saved before baptism?" Or perhaps, "Is the 144,000 a literal number?" I guarantee you this will heat things up. Just remember to generate more light than heat, and turn to God's Word for the answers.

4. Pray for revival. Mary and Martha prayed for Lazarus when he was dying and wept when he was dead. Jesus resurrected him. One thing we can always do in a dead church is to pray for a resurrection!

Surviving boring sermons

When people are asked why they feel their church is cold or dead, they often blame the pastor. "The sermons seem so lifeless and dull." There are two reasons the worship services can become routine, formal, and boring.

The first reason is the pastor; the second reason is the people.

Let's start by picking on the pastor. The best sermons I hear spring from the fresh experience of the person speaking. When Peter preached on Pentecost, he had no notes before him on the pulpit. I'm not saying that having notes is a sign of a bad sermon; it's just that Peter's words flowed from a heart that had just experienced forgiveness and an outpouring of the Holy Spirit.

We all need a daily experience in the things of God in order to have a fresh supply of inspiration to share with others, and pastors are no exception. So obviously, one thing we can do is to pray for our pastors instead of *preying* on them. Make sure they have plenty of time for study and sermon preparation by not bringing every little concern to them that someone else may be able to handle just as well.

Then the twelve said, "It is not reason that we should leave the word of God, and serve tables . . . but we will give ourselves continually to prayer, and to the ministry of the word" (Acts 6:2-4).

If you read an inspiring book, share it with your pastor. Though you probably won't hear a sermon about it the next week, your pastor may appreciate having a source of fresh ideas and variety. Knowing what interests the congregation is a key to having more relevant and interesting sermons.

Now, let's pick on the people. I know it's hard to listen to a boring sermon. But, speaking from the pastor's perspective, sometimes I've had to preach to boring congregations.

While visiting in a large city, I was asked to preach at two different churches on the same day. One was a suburban church of mostly Caucasian members, and the other was an ethnic black church. At the first church, the people just sat there politely, with no response or facial expressions. I did my best, but it seemed to be only an average delivery.

But when I went to the black church, the people didn't just sit there. They participated in the preaching. There was always some kind of response to whatever was being said. You could hear "Hallelujah," "Amen," or "Preach it, brother" throughout the whole sermon.

A friend once told me about an occasion when he was struggling through a sermon in a black church, and things weren't going too well. He was having trouble finding the right words. But he was encouraged when he heard the elders behind him on the platform saying, "Help him, Lord; help him!"

There was a different dynamic in the black church for me too. I got excited about what I was saying. Same sermon, but two different churches. I wasn't bored with the audience.

We think we're bored with the preacher, but could it be the preacher is bored with the people? If we were a better audience, perhaps the preacher would be more inspired! Let your pastor know you are listening by getting involved; respond to his sermon. Some positive feedback is like a breath of fresh air.

If that doesn't work, don't give up and drop out. No one should say they don't go to church because they are bored with the sermons. If nothing else, how often do you get quiet time to read the Bible? While you're sitting down for that thirty to forty minutes and the preacher is droning on and the elders on the platform are snoring, you could be quietly getting in a nice Bible study.

Some people may say, "I don't get anything out of church." This is another problem. Americans are TV-oriented. They are used to being entertained. But, there's no participation when you watch TV. You just sit there and soak it up. We come to church with the same attitude, expecting to be entertained, when, in reality, church should be where we go to give. We give our praise, our songs, our offering, our service, our attention to God and seek to hear His voice. No, there won't be any "pew potatoes" in heaven.

If we would just get out of this rut of thinking that a church is a "gimme, gimme" experience, we wouldn't come away saying we didn't get anything out of it. We would come away thanking the Lord we were able to give our praise and worship to Him.

One evangelist who was asked to give his response to a rather dull church service simply responded, "The speaker wasn't very interesting, but God sure was."

This brings out the core reason people are bored with their pastor's sermons. A heart that is void of the Holy Spirit will seldom have an appetite for spiritual food. But if we were hungering and thirsting after righteousness and the Word of God, we then would look past the faults of the pastor's sermon delivery and focus on the picture instead of the paintbrush. "To the hungry soul every bitter thing is sweet" (Proverbs 27:7).

Ellen White puts it this way:

While the people are so destitute of God's Holy Spirit, they cannot appreciate the preaching of the Word; but when the Spirit's power touches their hearts, then the discourses given will not be without effect (*Selected Messages*, 1:121).

Unfortunately, some pastors think the only solution for building church attendance is to break out the band and bring on the dancing deacons. If your pastor seems to be floundering for solutions for church attendance, perhaps he needs your help. Let him know you're on his side and that you want the church to be alive and growing.

The best way to energize a dead church is to invite some nonmembers to attend with you or to win some new converts who will have that "first love" coursing through their veins!

But many people say, "I'm embarrassed to invite anyone to our church. It's so cold the arctic air enshrouds you as soon as you walk through the door!"

You'd be surprised, but new converts or sincere people who visit your church hungering and thirsting after God will not so quickly notice the imperfections that are obvious to you. Rather, they will help you to get a fresh perspective.

One of the features of the body of Christ is that it constantly needs fresh transfusions of new converts to be healthy. The church must always be involved in evangelism to remain warm and vibrant. We are often caught in that vicious cycle of thinking our church is not ready for new people, when, in reality, new people are the cure.

So, would you like the formula for revival in a cold church?

1. Go home and get a piece of chalk.

2. Draw a circle three feet in diameter on the floor.

3. Kneel in the middle of the circle.

4. Pray that God will start a revival in that circle.

When God starts a revival in that circle, a revival will have begun in your church. Let your prayer be, "Lord, send a revival, and let it begin with me!"

When revival happens, you may face new problems. Your church may grow so rapidly, you may be wondering how you can ever survive in a big church.

Chapter 3

Surviving in a Big Church

Thou shalt not follow a multitude to do evil (Exodus 23:2, KJV).

You know you are in a big church when:

> . . . they release white pigeons at the end of every church service.

> . . . the pastor is asked to sign the guest book because most of the members don't get close enough to him to recognize him.

> . . . they call the song leader the minister of music.

> . . . it takes a week for gossip to circulate.

> . . . a shuttle bus takes you from the parking lot to the sanctuary.

After the divorce, Shirley knew she would need to go back to work to make ends meet. That meant moving to a larger city. Gopherhole was a nice little town, and the church was friendly, but there were very few job opportunities in such a remote community.

She had friends in Megamont City, and certainly there would be lots of work in that large metropolis, she thought. Once, while visiting there, she had visited the Megamont SDA Church. They had a beautiful, large facility with hundreds of members.

25

That's what she wanted, a new start with a new job, a new home, and especially some new friends who could help her through this painful time in her life.

After all the stress of moving to Megamont, Shirley was looking forward to her first Sabbath at the beautiful Megamont church. Upon arriving, she wondered if she had the right day. It was 9:45 a.m., and the enormous parking lot was nearly empty! She later learned that because city Christians are so busy during the week, about half the members sleep in and don't go to Sabbath School but only come for the later service.

At the entrance of the church, she was greeted by a friendly woman who gave her a bulletin, a smile, and one mechanical handshake. Shirley was disappointed that she couldn't talk to her a little more to find out about the church. She wanted to explain that she was new in town, but the friendly woman had to turn her attention to the line of people flowing in behind her.

As she entered the huge sanctuary, she felt like a minnow dropped into the Pacific Ocean. She quickly slid into one of the back pews in order not to look conspicuous but then realized she would need a pair of binoculars to see the front. "I'll just look through the bulletin until class starts," Shirley thought. The sermon title that day was "The Cosmic Prophetic Energy of God," by Pastor Phil O. Sophical.

"Hmm, sounds pretty deep," she decided.

Her thoughts were interrupted by a splendid voice singing a beautiful song, accompanied by the church string ensemble. Shirley was impressed, but at the same time realized she probably would not be asked to sing in the Megamont Church. Back in Gopherhole, if you could hum or whistle, it was good enough for special music.

Shirley quickly perceived that things would be different here. On the back of the bulletin, she noticed that the monthly church operating budget was $20,000. "I can see my meager offerings won't add up to much," she realized. Then she gazed around and saw the fine clothes everyone seemed to be wearing. By comparison, Shirley felt as if it appeared she did all her shopping at the thrift store.

She met some nice people at the Megamont Church, but she only saw them on Sabbath. Back in Gopherhole, you would see the church members all week long at the post office, at the market, at the school, or even at the gas station. There always seemed to be an opportunity to visit awhile. But Megamont City was so big that you could go for weeks without running into a familiar face.

After a few months, Shirley noticed that most of her friends were her neighbors in her apartment complex and her co-workers at the office. They were nice people. Some were Christians, but none of them were Adventist Christians.

Then one day, Shirley was invited to the office Halloween party on a Friday evening. She knew it wouldn't be good to go to a Halloween party, especially on Sabbath, but her hunger for friends was so strong that she went anyway. Other than a nagging conscience, Shirley had a good time and stayed out until 1:00 a.m.

Sabbath morning when the alarm went off, she felt so tired

and guilty, she simply turned off the alarm and rolled over. Hunkering down to sleep, she eased her conscience with the thought, "No one at the church will even notice I'm missing. No one there even cares about me." So, as Shirley drifted off to sleep, she drifted out of the church.

Sometimes, people in a big church don't know where they fit in. They don't feel needed or wanted. They feel uninvolved.

On the other hand, some people go to a big church so they can hide, usually to nurse some emotional wound or to cover up some sin in their life. They don't want anyone to get too close to them. They shut people out and cut off their very source of healing support.

In both cases, they often turn elsewhere for fellowship or leave the church entirely. The solution for both is to get involved.

Practical ways to survive in a big church

1. Take the initiative. Reach out to other people in the church. Some people complain they have no friends, but the problem is they're not being a friend. The Bible puts it this way, "A man who has friends must himself be friendly" (Proverbs 18:24). Try greeting newcomers or sitting by someone else who seems to be lost in the crowd too. If you want to have friends, you must be a friend.

2. Make your needs known. If you have needs, such as for counseling, Bible study, or even practical necessities, make them known to the church by being your own advocate. Most large churches have pastoral staff members or lay leaders who can take care of counseling needs. Often, they are just waiting to be able to do their job of ministering to those in need. Even in a small church, the pastor is often the last person to know when someone has experienced a tragedy or has a special need, because some people are too afraid or embarrassed to tell him. They just assume he will find out somehow. If you don't know how to locate someone to help you, a good place to start is by getting a copy of the church directory or the list of officers from the bulletin.

3. Don't let the size of the church overwhelm you. You may not be able to know and love each member of the entire church, but you can start with your Sabbath School class. Try inviting a few class members to your home for lunch or sundown worship on a Sabbath evening.

4. Sit up front. Remember, the church is only as large as the people sitting in front of you. If you feel like a lone minnow in a school of sardines, just swim up the aisle closer to shore, where you are less likely to drown in a sea of distractions. I've noticed at my evangelistic meetings that the ones who sit up front are the same ones who are baptized. Any teacher will tell you it is usually the "A" students who sit in the front of the class.

5. Participate whenever there is an opportunity. This may seem obvious, but you would be surprised how few people participate. Try going to the midweek prayer meeting. The size of the crowd is usually not so overwhelming, and the atmosphere is much more congenial, like being part of a family. If the church is conducting an evangelistic series, ask how you can help. Nothing will revive your faith faster than watching and helping new people come to Jesus!

6. Get involved. Break the habit of just being a pew warmer. Find out who is in charge of whatever department or program you have an interest in, and let them know you want to be involved. They would be overwhelmed if you volunteered your services. If they should seem too busy to notice you, be persistent. One woman at a Vacation Bible School workshop really brought this home to me when she said that she personally called over fifty people from her large church trying to get helpers for VBS, and not one person said Yes.

7. Start a church within a church. Find other members who share your desire for revival and burden for soul winning. Then meet together for singing, prayer, Bible study, and witnessing programs. In this way, you become like a "wheel within a wheel" and overcome the big church syndrome.

Overall, the key to surviving in a big church is to become part of the family. Anything you can do to make your worship experience seem more like a family gathering will add to the feeling of belonging. It will seem more like you are in a small church.

But even small churches can have their problems.

Chapter 4

Surviving in a Small Church

Where two or three are gathered together in my name, there am I in the midst of them (Matthew 18:20, KJV).

You know you are in a small church when:

> . . . the front door and the back door are the same.

> . . . the pastor preaches the sermon at 9:30 a.m. so he can be at the big church at 11:00.

> . . . the piano only has forty-four keys that work.

> . . . the head deacon, head elder, and Sabbath School superintendent are the same person.

> . . . when all the members of the board are from one family.

The Zeal family had moved to Podunk Valley twenty years earlier, before there was an SDA church there. They faithfully labored through the years as missionaries, giving Bible studies, health programs, and prophecy seminars until they raised up a company of believers. They later formed a small church with a whopping membership of forty-five.

In time, some of the new members began to feel that the Zeal family had too much control of their little church. After all, Mr. Zeal was head elder, Mrs. Zeal was Sabbath School superintendent and head deaconess. Homer Zeal, their thirty-year-old son, was head deacon and Sabbath School teacher. His unmarried sister, Prudence Zeal, was Dorcas leader, organist, and, of course, communication secretary. So, the church board meetings looked something like a family reunion.

Because the Podunk Church was so small, they didn't have a full-time pastor. One of the associate pastors from Megamont City Church came to preach every other week. Hence, most of the problems and decisions were handled by Elder Zeal. He was a good man, but he felt his way was the only way, and the Podunk Church was his church.

If one of the new members was missing on Sabbath morning, Mr. Zeal would call first thing on Sunday morning and ask with an air of suspicion, "Is everything all right?"

To his way of thinking, catastrophic illness was the only good reason not to attend church (I tend to agree with Mr. Zeal on this point), and some folks resented his attitude.

One evening when Prudence Zeal was driving by the house of Loretta Loose, one of the new but weaker members, she noticed a strange man walking in the door. Early the next morning, Prudence "just happened" to drive by again and noticed the man's car still parked there.

Out of a sincere desire to save Loretta from a life of sin, Prudence called each of the other church members and, with a concerned voice, explained the apparent problem while including a few imaginary details. She then asked them to pray for Loretta. After the rumor had thoroughly circulated and made its way back to Loretta, the truth came out. "The mystery man" was Loretta's brother visiting from Megamont.

As you can see, one of the problems generally facing a small church is the overinvolvement of fellow members in each other's lives. There is sometimes too much meddling in people's private business. There also seems to be a hesitancy to let new-comers be integrated into meaningful church leadership, even if the "newcomer" has been a faithful member there for fifteen years.

Often, the reason why there is a power struggle for leadership within a small church is that all the leadership roles are

tied up in one family like the Zeals.

Perhaps it was just such a family Ellen White wrote about when God inspired her to pen these words:

It is not the best policy for children of one, two, or three families that are connected by marriage, to settle within a few miles of one another. The influence is not good on the parties. The business of one is the business of all. The perplexities and troubles which every family must experience more or less, and which, as far as possible, should be confined within the limits of the family circle, are extended to family connections, and have a bearing upon the religious meetings. . . . That dignity, that high regard, confidence, and love that make a prosperous church is not preserved. All parties would be much happier to be separated and to visit occasionally, and their influence upon one another would be tenfold greater (*Testimonies for the Church*, 3:55).

Tips for surviving in a small church

1. Respect the privacy of other members, and guard the privacy of your own home. After all, this is just following the Golden Rule: "Just as you want men to do to you, you also do to them likewise" (Luke 6:31). Though there may be nothing to hide, every family needs its privacy.

Oh, how many lives are made bitter by the breaking down of the walls which inclose the privacies of every family, and which are calculated to preserve its purity and sanctity! (*The Adventist Home*, 337).

Remember to give people their due space, and graciously make sure to let them know when you need yours.

2. Refuse to be a link in the gossip chain. When people come to you with a juicy story, you don't have to listen. Try ignoring their stories and encouraging them to pray for the individual rather than talk badly about him or her. Remember, don't be a link in the chain—don't pass the story on.

3. Try not to play favorites. Although it may be a temptation to try to get in with the "in crowd," remember that Jesus was the friend of outcasts. He treated both John and Judas with equal love and respect.

4. Don't get into a power struggle for church leadership. People who cling to power usually do so from a point of weakness rather than strength. A person who is truly strong in the Lord will not feel threatened by others and will give them an opportunity to exercise their gifts and talents. On the other hand, people who are truly gifted don't necessarily need to be in leadership in order to exercise their gifts. They won't mind if someone else gets the credit or the leadership role.

5. Search for hidden gifts. In a small church, it's usually the same few people who always do certain things. This is partly due to some wanting to maintain control. But more often, it is because the same people are always asked, and the willing workers are being worn out. Naturally, in a small church, there is a smaller pool of talent from which to pick. But if the leaders are willing to take a risk from time to time, they might discover undeveloped gifts and hidden talents right in their midst. Because Loretta didn't have a piano in her house, no one thought to ask her if she could play, yet she played beautifully. Because George Alexander was blind, folk thought they needed to pamper this "handicapped member." But by using Braille and cassettes, George always did a complete study of the Sabbath School lesson. He made a terrific Sabbath School teacher.

6. Add some new enthusiasm. Sometimes a church is small because its witnessing program is stunted and needs a transfusion of new members. As I mentioned earlier, the church must always be involved in evangelism to remain warm and vibrant. If the rest of the church members are more interested in maintaining the status quo than in praying for revival, you can have a one-man or one-woman evangelistic series by witnessing for Christ and giving personal Bible studies.

The only drawback to winning new converts to Christ is that it makes the devil mad, and he will seek to discourage them.

Chapter 5

Surviving as a New Member

By one Spirit are we all baptized into one body, whether we be Jews or Gentiles, whether we be bond or free; and have been all made to drink into one Spirit (1 Corinthians 12:13, KJV).

You know you are a new member when:

> . . . you bring Kentucky Fried Chicken to the church potluck.

> . . . you think Ingathering means having your trousers taken in at the waist.

> . . . you think foot washing means cleaning a ruler.

> . . . you read in the Bible that God can move mountains, and you believe it.

Haley was the perfect target of the evangelistic crusade. She began attending meetings after receiving a flyer in the mail and seemed genuinely interested in the lessons. The visitation teams commented, "She'd make a great member if we could just get her to stop smoking."

"And take off those dangling earrings," one said.

Another piped in, "She makes a good salary too. I know her offerings could really help the building fund."

As the meetings progressed, the teams made weekly stops at Haley's home, encouraging her to continue coming and urging her to make a decision for baptism. Haley didn't want to be rude to her guests but wasn't sure she was quite ready to take "the plunge." That didn't stop them. They rushed to the evangelist. "She's so close to making a decision. Why don't you and the pastor stop by to see her?"

A few days later, Haley found herself sitting in the audience of the crusade meetings while the evangelist made the call for "all those who want to follow Jesus in obedience" to come forward in commitment to be baptized. The evangelist seemed to be looking straight at her. She tried averting her eyes to avoid his gaze.

"If only I could quit smoking," she thought to herself. Suddenly, she felt her body moving forward as she heard the evangelists words, "This may be your last chance; don't wait any longer." The next morning found Haley, still smelling like smoke from her last cigarette, lined up with ninety-six other candidates awaiting baptism in the academy swimming pool after the Sabbath-morning services.

All that week Haley chewed gum, ate carrots, and gnawed on her pencil, doing whatever she could to avoid smoking, and she was successful, that is, until Friday night. Sabbath morning she woke up drowning in remorse for giving in to temptation, but she thought, "Everyone has been so nice to me at church; I don't want to let them down," so she dressed and got ready for church.

The former visitation teams had turned into inspection teams and were out in full force that first Sabbath after the big baptism. Hair combed? Check. Earrings absent? Check. Bible in hand? Yep.

The mental tally went on as the new members ran the gauntlet through the foyer. Of course, their conversation was cordial. "Welcome to Sabbath School," they greeted each one passing inspection. When Haley walked through the door, she relaxed as she was greeted warmly until she reached Mrs. Bizzi.

"Why, Haley, you smell just like a tobacco factory. You must live near someone who smokes, dear," Mrs. Bizzi blurted loudly across the foyer.

"Umm, I . . . I stopped to visit my next-door neighbor before I left for church, and she's a chain smoker," Haley offered weakly and went in to find a seat. Haley sat uneasily during the service and rushed out during the closing hymn to avoid shaking everyone's hand on her way out.

During the next week, she tried chewing on carrots again but only made it to Thursday without smoking. On Sabbath morning, she decided she couldn't stand the thought of going to church and having to lie about her smoking, so she stayed home to read her Bible. But even that made her feel guilty, so she picked up a magazine instead. Soon she found herself staring at a cigarette ad and started looking for her matches. As she lit up, her good intentions to follow Jesus went up in smoke.

Though all may not have a problem with smoking, the good intentions of many newly baptized members often go up in flames. They feel rushed into a decision to follow Jesus before they really know what it means to be a disciple.

Sometimes, people who once seemed encouraging and supportive to them before their baptism now seem faultfinding and cold. The Sabbath School lessons are not as easy to follow as the evangelist's presentations, and new believers begin to slip between the cracks. They are stuck between the worldly lifestyle they want to leave behind and knowing how to follow Jesus all the way in the new Christian lifestyle.

As an evangelist, I have noticed that during a series of meetings, the new interests are showered with love and attention. But after an interest is baptized, there is a tendency to think, "Well, we caught that fish." Then we leave them to die and dry on the beach while we move on to other projects.

If you are newly baptized, don't give up! You are at the perfect place to begin learning how to survive in church. You are actually where a lot more of us need to be, back at the beginning, still remembering your first love. From here, you can begin to establish those habits that will keep you from falling into the cracks if you will turn to God for help.

Jude wrote that Jesus "is able to keep you from falling, and to present you faultless before the presence of his glory with exceeding joy" (Jude 24). So, if Jesus knows how to do that, He can help you to survive in church.

If you have wandered away from Jesus back into your former life, Jesus says, "Remember therefore from whence thou art fallen, and repent, and do the first works" (Revelation 2:5). Begin again to follow Jesus. Don't worry about being rejected. Jesus said, "All that the Father giveth me shall come to me; and him that cometh to me I will in no wise cast out" (John 6:37). As long as you are willing to repent, He is willing to forgive (1 John 1:9; Matthew 18:21, 22).

The apostle Paul wrote, "I die daily" (1 Corinthians 15:31), signifying that each one of us needs a daily conversion experience. But don't stop there. If you die daily without being born again daily, then you are more dead than alive! (You have probably met people like that.) It's not enough to be crucified with Christ and buried; we must also rise with Him to live a new life.

Ellen White makes this suggestion:

Consecrate yourself to God in the morning; make this your very first work. Let your prayer be, "Take me, O Lord, as wholly Thine. I lay all my plans at Thy feet. Use me to-day in Thy service. Abide with me, and let all my work be wrought in Thee." This is a daily matter. Each morning consecrate yourself to God for that day. Surrender all your plans to Him, to be carried out or given up as His providence shall indicate. Thus day by day you may be giving your life into the hands of God, and thus your life will be molded more and more after the life of Christ (*Steps to Christ*, 70).

Early in my ministry I had the sad task of performing a funeral for a family who lost their three-month-old baby. One morning when they came to the crib, the baby was still and cold. He had just stopped breathing some time during the night. They call this "crib death." I have witnessed many new members experience a spiritual crib death. They lose their eternal life early in their new birth simply because they stop breathing in prayer or eating Bible bread.

Spending time in God's Word and in prayer is essential to living the Christian life. Pray especially for the Holy Spirit. It's His job to show you how to live. Jesus said of the Holy Spirit, "When He, the Spirit of truth, has come, He will guide you into all truth" (John 16:13).

Remember to keep your focus on Christ and not on other people. You should live a life that people can look at, but don't you be looking at people as your example. Look to Christ. When Peter wanted to know what Jesus was going to do with the apostle John, Jesus essentially told Peter to mind his own business. He said, "If I will that he remain till I come, what is that to you? follow You me" (John 21:22). Certainly we can pray for other people and be concerned for their well-being, but our focus and our efforts need to be on following Christ ourselves.

A good beginning is to establish habits of prayer and Bible study, as I have mentioned over and over again. If you don't know where to start, start at the bookstore. There are dozens of good books on all the basic how-tos of prayer and Bible study. Psalm 55:17 sets a good pattern: "Evening, and morning, and at noon, will I pray, and cry aloud: and he shall hear my voice" (KJV).

Another habit that needs to be cultivated is learning how to keep the Sabbath as it should be kept—holy. You might want to try asking a few older members how they keep the Sabbath. If they have been at this for so many years that they don't remember having any problems figuring out what to do on long Sabbath afternoons, try asking a family with young children how they have tackled this challenge. Just make sure you check out their ideas to make sure they line up with the Bible so you won't be following human ideas instead of God's.

Mitzi listened to her sister tell all about the Sabbath being a day when you get to do all those things you don't normally get to do during the week. "Great," she thought, "finally I will get a chance to go shopping!"

It wasn't until her car broke down three Sabbaths in a row

(but ran fine during the week) that she realized the Lord must be trying to get her attention. Then she read the text about not buying or selling on the Sabbath (Nehemiah 10:31).

The two things a new member needs to remember most are these: the journey of a thousand miles begins with a single step, and attack can be expected along the way.

Remember that right after Jesus' baptism, the devil met Him in the wilderness to discourage Him from His mission. Now that you have taken that first step toward Jesus in baptism, keep on going in that direction. If you stumble, ask the Lord for help to get back up and keep going. If others try to trip you up, remind them that you are on a journey and a march, and you are going as fast as you can. Invite them to pray for you rather than to criticize you. And remember that one of the best ways to keep moving forward is to invite others along for the ride through sharing your faith.

Some people think that life will be a bed of roses once they are baptized into Christ, and in some ways, it is. You just have to remember that roses grow on thorn bushes! When you accept Christ as your Lord and Saviour, you turn traitor to Satan's army and become his target. Things may have seemed easier for you before your baptism than they seem afterward. That is because before you were baptized, Satan didn't have to put as much effort into getting you to be on his side. After all, you were born there.

The attack often begins just after your baptism. That's when Satan tempted Christ, and we should expect no less. The point of my telling you this is not to frighten or discourage you but to warn you so you can brace yourself and be prepared. You prepare by fortifying your mind with Scripture and praying for divine help every day.

By forming the habits of worship, prayer and study, and keeping focused on Christ instead of on people or circumstances, new members can learn to survive in church. But when the devil fails to discourage you as a new Christian, he often resorts to plan B and distracts you with internal divisions.

Chapter 6

Surviving in a Divided Church

I plead with you, brethren, by the name
of our Lord Jesus Christ, that you all speak the
same thing, and that there be no divisions among
you, but that you be perfectly joined together
in the same mind and in the same judgment
(1 Corinthians 1:10).

You know you are in a divided church when:

- . . . the left half of the church carpet is orange, and the right half is blue.

- . . . campaign and election posters appear in the foyer before the nominating committee meets.

- . . . people come to church driving army tanks.

- . . . flashing red and blue lights appear in front of the church after every board meeting.

The first time I ever preached a sermon in a church, I was a recovering hippie fresh out of the woods. If you have read the book *The Richest Caveman: The Doug Batchelor Story*, you know there was a time when I never wore clothes. I felt I was doing the people a big favor by trading in my overalls and putting on a jacket to preach. But I simply refused to wear a necktie!

One of the things that appealed to me about the Seventh-day

Adventist Church was that it's beliefs were so rational and practical. However, I couldn't think of any practical reason for wearing a tie. It doesn't hold your shirt on the way a belt holds up your pants, and a tie chokes you! Not to mention, you have to think about whether or not it matches the rest of your outfit, and I have little sense of taste. (My wife says it's improving.)

So, I preached in the Covelo church, tieless. Even though I was terrified, the people seemed to be blessed with the message. However, before we all left the church foyer that day, one of the saints said, "Doug, you really should wear a tie when you preach up front."

"Why?" I responded.

Someone else said, "He doesn't need a tie to preach."

"When we go before God, we should be more respectful," the first saint returned.

"Where does the Bible say that?" someone else joined in.

Soon the foyer was buzzing, debating the issue of ties in the pulpit! By the next weekend, the loving members of my little church were evenly divided over whether to tie or not to tie. And, because of my stubborn pride, I was helping fuel the fire!

I know it sounds ridiculous, but I've seen some churches plunge into civil war over the color of the carpet, the new organ, or whether a man should grow a beard to get to heaven. I'll admit that there are some dividing issues that are more serious— such as pastoral conduct or doctrinal standards—but for whatever reason, divided churches are a problem.

First, let's distinguish a "divided" church from the normal disagreements Christian brothers and sisters will encounter. A church is divided when disagreement cripples or distracts the church from fulfilling its gospel mission. For example, when issues begin to take energy and attention that should be devoted to reaching the lost and reviving the members, then there is division in the church.

As Christians, Jesus has called us to love our enemies. But many professed Christians can't even love their spouses, let alone love their fellow believers.

Jesus tells us, "By this all will know that you are My disciples, if you have love for one another" (John 13:35).

The devil knows that if a church's love and unity attracts people, then division will repel them. So he works to divide. The church is the body of Christ, and when a body is divided, it cannot function well. The life span of an arm or leg divided from the rest of the body is very short.

So, how do you survive in a divided church?

For one thing, work to keep your priorities in order. Do not allow insignificant or trivial issues, like ties, to sap the energy of your church family. I have seen many churches divided over issues that are big on earth but petty in the eyes of heaven.

> Woe to you, scribes and Pharisees, hypocrites! For you pay tithe of mint and anise and cummin, and have neglected the weightier matters of the law: justice and mercy and faith (Matthew 23:23).

As far as possible, without sacrificing Christian principles, don't take sides. We can see many examples in Scripture where Jesus refused to become entangled in trivial, divisive issues because they would distract from His mission.

> Then one from the crowd said to Him, "Teacher, tell my brother to divide the inheritance with me." But He said to him, "Man, who made Me a judge or an arbitrator over you?" (Luke 12:13, 14).

Not taking sides doesn't mean inactivity, though. You can and should pray for unity. We sometimes view prayer as a spiritual bandage or a nice gesture. In reality, prayer is the most powerful tool the Lord has given us. One of Jesus' last prayers was for the disciples to be united as one.

He prayed:

> "I do not pray for these alone, but also for those who will believe in Me through their word; that they all may be one,

as You, Father, are in Me, and I in You; that they also may be one in Us, that the world may believe that You sent Me. And the glory which You gave Me I have given them, that they may be one just as We are one: I in them, and You in Me; that they may be made perfect in one, and that the world may know that You have sent Me, and have loved them as You have loved Me (John 17:20-23).

Your words and actions should remind your brothers and sisters what the Christian priorities are: first, to know God, His love, and His salvation; second, to help other people know God and His love and salvation. In other words, choose to be part of the answer instead of the problem. "Blessed are the peace-makers: for they shall be called the children of God" (Matthew 5:9).

At this point, I should mention that in every Christian church, just like earthly families, there will be disagreements. Sometimes we must simply agree to disagree and to work side by side. Nonetheless, a Christian should never be disagreeable. Any disagreements should be discussed with a kind and loving Christian spirit or not at all.

It helps to remember that God can turn every situation to His advantage, even division in the church. "We know that in all things, God works for the good of those who love Him" (Romans 8:28, NIV).

The Bible tells us that the missionary team of Paul and Barnabas had such a strong disagreement that they picked different partners, formed two teams, and went in different directions. Rather than ending in disaster, their division resulted in spreading the gospel to more people as they each worked in their own way. The Lord blessed both teams.

Many church divisions have resulted in two churches where there had formerly been one. There is nothing wrong with this if the church divides with a loving spirit to create more room for others. Or if it divides to give an option to those who may feel more comfortable worshiping in a slightly different way.

One of the main things we need to learn as Christians is to

love. We all have love problems. God wants us to learn to love Him more, and in so doing, to love one another more. The way we learn anything is by experience. In many cases, when we have disagreements, it is because we have had different experiences.

Just take, for example, the story of Timmy, a boy who went to kindergarten and tried hard to be a model student. One day, the teacher passed around papers and asked the children to color the pictures of flowers, apples, and pigs. Timmy took out his crayons and began to color. For the flowers, he used red and green crayons. He colored the apple yellow. Timmy worked the hardest on the pig, which he colored white with black spots.

Soon the teacher came around to collect the papers, and when she got to Timmy, she just stopped and said in disappointment, "Don't you know that apples are red? Everyone knows that pigs aren't black and white; they're pink."

Timmy tried to explain his color choices to the teacher, but she didn't have time to listen. Timmy knew better than to argue with his teacher, so he never went back to kindergarten at that school. Instead, he stayed home and ate yellow delicious apples and watched the black-and-white Hampshire pigs in the neighbor's yard next door.

Who was right, Timmy or his teacher? The real answer is both and neither. Both were right about the color of apples and pigs. There are both red and yellow apples, both pink and black-and-white pigs. They both could have benefited from the other's experience.

Unfortunately, both were also wrong. The teacher was wrong to be harsh and close minded in her attitude toward Timmy. The teacher could have had a model student if she had been willing to learn from the experience of one of her pupils. However, Timmy was wrong in letting it keep him out of kindergarten.

My point is, be willing to learn from the experiences of others, and consider a different perspective. Too often, churches will disagree out of lack of experience. Both sides may be right in the view they espouse, but both may be wrong in their attitudes.

Rather, the church should be like a sensitive, tolerant, loving family.

The reason God places people in families is so we can learn to love. Even in healthy families, there are conflicts and differences, but they are seasoned with love. When a brother and sister have an argument, they don't say, "I'm leaving the family."

But this is what happens in many church families. People have a disagreement, and they say, "I don't want to be part of this church family anymore, because I'm angry or I've been hurt by someone or they're mad at me." We need to manifest more of a family commitment in our church and do everything possible to reconcile our differences.

One of the best ways to learn to love is by being around people who are not always loving and lovable. You don't learn anything without resistance. Your muscles don't get strong through rest, but strengthen through strain. Our love muscles and faith muscles develop when our faith is tried, and we are exposed to unlovable people. This is another reason a church environment is so important.

If Jesus were walking the earth today, would you want to be with Him and with the twelve apostles? I think your answer would be Yes. Remember, Jesus had a Judas in His church who was doing things wrong. Even though the Lord knew it, He did not expose him.

Peter, James, and John were arguing among themselves for the highest position. Through their conflict and through their division, they were learning to love each other. By the time the Day of Pentecost came, they had sincerely put away their differences. They were able to kneel together, and pray together in the same place, and God was able to pour out His Spirit (Acts 1:14).

This will also have to happen to us before we receive the outpouring of the Holy Spirit. We must learn to speak together, pray together, and put aside our differences.

If you are faced with division, you need to affirm your commitment to truth, humble yourself, and bend all your efforts toward reconciliation. This is done through seeking the Lord's will and going on with the mission of bringing souls to Christ.

Surviving when there is division

1. Avoid taking sides. We should always stand for truth and call sin by its right name. But most church divisions are not over what is right or wrong. Churches split over power, influence, personal preference, or pride. You can avoid division by remembering that the Scriptures say: "Let nothing be done through selfish ambition or conceit, but in lowliness of mind let each esteem others better than himself" (Philippians 2:3).

2. Put it all into perspective. Ask, "Is this really worth it?" There's no use hassling over the small stuff (like ties). Ask yourself if this will really matter, really make any difference, in five years or twenty years or in eternity. If it won't, then it will only serve to distract you from doing the Lord's will. It isn't worth fighting about.

3. Be willing to consider both points of view. Romans 14:5 says, "Let each be fully convinced in his own mind." In order to be persuaded, you must objectively listen to the reasoning of each side. Though the best advice is to stay out of an argument, this tactic may be used when others are already divided, and you get dragged into it. Sometimes, in just explaining a point of view and having to answer honest questions, the one in the wrong may develop a more positive perspective and see another point of view.

4. Seek counsel. The Bible says, "Where no counsel is, the people fall: but in the multitude of counsellors there is safety" (Proverbs 11:14).

It is easy to be swayed into sin if you are following the opinions of one person. Ask the advice of other experienced and objective Christians. Of course, your first source of counsel should be God's Word. After all, Jesus' name is "Wonderful, Counselor" (Isaiah 9:6).

5. Set a good example. Don't get involved in senseless controversy. Strive toward reconciliation. If you are a participant in the division, be willing to admit when you are wrong.

Matthew 5:23-26 outlines the steps to take:

a. If you have been wronged, seek reconciliation immediately. Stewing in your juices only makes you boil over down the road. You cannot have the right relationship with God while you are harboring an unforgiving spirit toward someone else.

"If you forgive men their trespasses, your heavenly Father will also forgive you. But if you do not forgive men their trespasses, neither will your Father forgive your trespasses" (Matthew 6:14, 15).

b. If you are in the wrong, honestly try to make things right before the wronged party has to come looking for you. If you try to avoid him, you only prolong the argument and intensify it.

6. If a conflict cannot be resolved, agree to disagree. Let your disagreement allow inclusion and growth rather than exclusion and division.

If we can learn to handle conflict and division in the church with the Spirit of Christ, our churches can become like a big family with a loving magnetism.

Some people will get plenty of practice at this because they have to know how to survive in a divided home too.

Chapter 7

Surviving in Church With a Divided Home

A man's foes shall be they of his own household (Matthew 10:36, KJV).

You know you are in a divided home when:

> ... one spouse reaches for the Bible while the other grabs *TV Guide*.

> ... the radio stations on the car radio are preset for rock and Christian stations.

> ... it takes twice as many pots and pans to prepare a meal.

Janice and Leroy had what many Americans would call an average lifestyle and a normal relationship. Leroy worked five days a week at the lumber mill, while Janice took care of the kids, the home, and the shopping. On Saturdays, the kids had Little League games, or the family went water-skiing. Saturday night, friends would come by and play cards and have a few beers. Sundays were reserved for sleeping in, mowing the lawn, or household projects, plus an occasional sporting event.

They weren't rich, but they were comfortable. Still, Janice was haunted by a feeling of emptiness. Something was missing. Life seemed so short. There must be more purpose to living

than paying off the car and the house, retiring, then picking a cemetery plot.

One day, Janice's friend Debbie came by with a handbill, advertising a Bible seminar at her church. Janice wasn't really interested, because Debbie had some kooky habits. It wasn't so much her vegetarian diet Janice objected to, but her going to church on Saturdays. She also wouldn't play cards with them, nor did she wear jewelry. Although Debbie had some strange beliefs, she also possessed an unusual kindness and persistence. "Just come one night," Debbie pleaded.

Janice couldn't say no, so Friday night found Leroy reluctantly watching the kids while Janice and Debbie "got some religion."

The young minister at the church seemed average in his build and appearance, but there was something extraordinary about the message. Janice could feel a strange hunger stirring inside her and a quiet voice telling her this was what was missing from her life.

The next morning, when Janice told Leroy she intended to attend all three weeks of the meetings, he nearly went through the roof. Then Janice asked him to go with her. He was insistent when he said, "If you want to get religious, that's up to you, but don't be preaching to me!"

Before the series of meetings was half over, Janice knew that she was hearing the truth and that Jesus was calling her, but she quickly saw that it was going to cause serious problems in her relationship with Leroy and the children. To be baptized and become a Bible-believing Christian would affect every area of her life—what she ate, what she wore, what she watched on TV, and how she spent her time and money. The problems seemed overwhelming, and Janice knew there would be tremendous conflict with Leroy. She also knew that if she would ever see her dear family saved, she would have to be the first one to make the step and cross over to Jesus.

At the conclusion of the meetings, Janice and four others were baptized. The singing was beautiful, the church was full, and it would have been the happiest day of her life if only Leroy had come.

The story just related is based on many true accounts of how a divided home can develop. Sadly, many divided homes are created by choice when a Seventh-day Adventist Christian willingly marries a nonbeliever in the hope that sometime he or she will be converted. Big mistake!

Sometimes these miracles will happen, but they are the exception, not the rule. Just for the record, if you are a Seventh-day Adventist thinking of marrying a person of another faith or one who has no religion, first spend some time talking to people who have made this decision. If you still think it's the right thing to do, you may not be very serious about your relationship with Jesus.

However, if you find yourself in a divided home by providence or by choice, how do you survive?

For one thing, do not consider divorce an option. As soon as you start thinking that way, you will subconsciously stop praying for the conversion of your spouse. I have seen many cases in which Christian partners deliberately made their spouses so miserable that they drove them away. Then they lamented, "I'm innocent. He [or she] just left me."

The Bible says:

> If any brother has a wife who does not believe, and she is willing to live with him, let him not divorce her. And a woman who has a husband who does not believe, if he is willing to live with her, let her not divorce him. For the unbelieving husband is sanctified by the wife, and the unbelieving wife is sanctified by the husband; otherwise your children would be unclean, but now they are holy. But if the unbeliever departs, let him depart; a brother or a sister is not under bondage in such cases. But God has called us to peace. For how do you know, O wife, whether you will save your husband? Or how do you know, O husband, whether you will save your wife? (1 Corinthians 7:12-16).

The problems that can develop in a divided home where one is a Seventh-day Adventist Christian and one is not can be as varied and diverse as the personalities involved. These problems can reach all the way from the kitchen to the bedroom and from the clothes in the closet to the car in the garage.

Practical ways to survive in a divided home without losing your faith or losing your mind.

1. Respect your spouse's freedom of choice. Remember that God never uses force to compel us to serve Him. In many cases, the unbelieving party feels pressure to change values and habits. This pressure usually produces stubborn opposition. Often, by nagging and playing mind games, the churchgoing spouse becomes the agent of the devil to permanently harden his or her partner's resistance. Let the Holy Spirit apply the pressure; He knows just how much and at what time it is best to poke the conscience. This simple respect will greatly reduce conflict. In other words, lead; don't push.

Part of respecting your spouse's freedom of choice is to remember, if your situation is like Janice and Leroy's, that your spouse did not choose to be married to a Christian. In effect, your spouse is living with a different person. If you were converted after your marriage, it is you who changed the rules of the game, so be considerate. Your spouse married a nonbeliever who was interested in doing things a nonbeliever does.

2. Choose your battles carefully. There are going to be conflicts, but as far as possible, without sacrificing any Christian principles, make compromises to demonstrate your willingness to have peace in the family.

For example, your unbelieving spouse wants to take you and the kids to the county fair on Sabbath. You might say, "Dear, I will be happy to go with you and the kids on Sunday. Can we please wait one day?"

Don't say, "You know that's the day I go to church. If you want to take the kids, you go right ahead, but you'll do it alone!" This will only create more conflict.

3. When a conflict does arise, pray, pray, pray. Then be careful not to use the devil's weapons to fight the Lord's battles. Use these disagreements as opportunities to show how the Lord has changed your life and heart. Don't allow yourself to revert to old patterns of yelling and screaming or even give the hint of losing your temper. This is just what the devil wants you to do, to give your partner reason to doubt the power of your religion.

Be careful never to compromise in the area of Christian standards, because it will be thrown back at you in times of conflict. Pray that the Lord will help you to be consistent.

In one study, rats were put into cages in which the food was either distributed only once an hour or distributed randomly, with a 10 percent chance of getting food. The rats with the hourly distribution soon learned not to waste their energy and only pushed the button for food once an hour. However, the rats in cages with the random feeding times spent all their energy and all their time pushing the button for food, even with only a one-in-ten chance they would get their way.

If you want your spouse to keep pushing your hot buttons in

the area of your faith, just give in to temptation every now and then.

4. Be a good example. If you have not been a good example of a Bible Christian, tell your spouse and kids, and ask for their forgiveness. This will clean the slate for a new start. Sometimes, just admitting that you don't think your faith has made you perfect and above reproach will let your spouse and kids up for air. It may even give them encouragement to realize they may be eligible for salvation too, if being perfect is not the first requirement.

The children

Having children in a divided home can surely complicate your life. How smoothly the relationship works will obviously depend on the tolerance and understanding of your mate. Daily worship with the children, the value of Christian education, attitudes about movie-going, TV-watching, Sabbath keeping, prayer before meals, not to mention the food on the table itself, can all be points of conflict.

Start by making sure that you are up front and open with your children. Assure them that Mommy and Daddy do love each other, but they feel differently about God. Make good use of every quiet moment alone with the children to teach them about Jesus and explain the plan of salvation. Hopefully, the unbelieving spouse will not resist your bringing the children to church or praying with them at home.

> It is the duty of Christian parents, morning and evening, by earnest prayer and persevering faith to make a hedge about their children (*Child Guidance*, 519).

Again, try to win them to Jesus by your example. Let them see that your faith makes you a better parent. This may mean apologizing for past mistakes.

Before you come down heavy-handed and quote Ephesians 6:1, "Children, obey your parents," read on, and take the advice of verse 4 to heart.

It reads:

> Now a word to you parents. Don't keep on scold-
> ing and nagging your children, making them angry and
> resentful. Rather, bring them up with the loving discipline
> the Lord himself approves, with suggestions and godly
> advice (Ephesians 6:4, TLB).

If you have not always been a Christian, remember that it will take time to instill Christian values in the hearts of your children and your spouse.

Finally, refuse to let the children set you up by pitting you against your spouse because they are aware of your opposing values. Rather, let them see that you and your mate stick together as parents, as far as possible. You must also see that the children are not used as a tool by your mate to coerce you into giving up your convictions or to drag you into an argument.

Perhaps you began reading this chapter knowing that you live in a divided home, but of a different sort. The division is not always between husband and wife but may be between parent and child, brother and sister, or even between roommates. These struggles can be equally as challenging.

Diane became a Christian while still living in her parents' home. They didn't oppose her decision, but the division did create stress that was difficult for all of them to live with. Sud-denly, the rules changed. Sabbath afternoons became stress filled as she stayed home instead of going shopping with her mother. She avoided the living room, where the TV was on.

At first, her parents were convinced it was just a phase she was going through. It seemed to Diane the baked ham her mother just happened to be serving one Sabbath afternoon was a little more than a coincidence. It seemed as if her parents presented every enticement they could to remind her how much more fun their lifestyle was than hers. And, who can blame them for trying? It was probably their way of convincing themselves they were OK and didn't need to join her by giving their lives to Christ. This is one way friends and family may subconsciously test you when you take a stand for Jesus.

The key is to walk as Jesus walked. If your opposition comes from parents, remember Scripture says to honor your father and mother. This means being obedient in every way you can and giving them respect. It does not mean obeying them above obeying your heavenly Father when these two duties conflict.

Living with opposition from other sources (parents, siblings, or roommates) calls for survival skills that are much the same as dealing with a spouse. The only benefit is that you are not married to your parents, siblings, or roommates, so you can eventually establish your own home. Then you'll only have to deal with holidays and family reunions!

Those of you with established homes may worry about visiting family members who are opposed to your faith. To make these times easier, try to establish guidelines beforehand. For instance, how often you will visit, for how long, and what activities you can do together are good topics to start with. If you have children, make sure that, when visiting, parents or grandparents agree to respect your values regarding the children. Grandparents are famous for unlimited candy, unrestricted TV, and spending sprees. This is one reason holidays can be a strain for Christian parents. Try establishing good communication with your family about holidays well in advance.

It is especially important to make every visit the object of special prayer. As the time draws near, pray that your faith will be strong, your witness positive, and that the Holy Spirit will be active. Pray not only that you will be ready to speak a word in due season but that the Holy Spirit will have gone before you to prepare your family to listen.

Maybe your family doesn't seem to be experiencing any of these divisions. Praise the Lord; you have a lot for which to be thankful if your spouse or your children are not constantly challenging your faith.

But let's talk more about children. Even if your kids do not oppose your faith or your parental authority, they may be bored with going to church. How do you survive? How do you keep your kids in church? Perhaps the next chapter can help.

Chapter 8

Surviving as Youth in Church

(what parents can do)

I will contend with him who contends with you, and I will save your children (Isaiah 49:25).

You know our young people are drifting out of church when:

> ... they start asking if Sabbath is over six hours before sundown.

> ... they have more non-Christian than Christian friends.

> ... they always ask, "What's wrong with ... ?"

> ... they always want to sit in the back of the church.

> ... they seldom listen to Christian music or read Christian books.

A story told about President Abraham Lincoln says that he was out taking a walk in a field to think and happened to meet a little girl about six years old. She didn't seem to know who he was. They had a nice, friendly chat, and she asked him if they could meet again the next day at one o'clock. He agreed and went back to the affairs of the nation.

The next day, an urgent request came from a head of state for the president to meet with him at one o'clock. The president replied that he could not, because he already had a pressing engagement. The president knew that there was no way of reaching the little girl, because he didn't even know her name or where to find her. As promised, he walked out to the field at one o'clock and had another nice visit with the little girl. He then returned again to his work of leading the country. Keeping his word to a six-year-old girl was more important to him than any urgent meeting.

Is this the message we are giving our young people? Do they know that they are very important to us? Are we letting them know they really count? Or are we telling them they are second-class people who just get in the way? If we want our young people to survive in church, we need to be able to answer these questions. Otherwise, the pews will continue to be empty.

This chapter deserves a whole book by itself, but I have tried to cut it down and just include some key points. The largest group of people who are struggling to survive in church are the youth. And they are the group with the greatest potential for Christ. I have heard varying percentages, but more than 50 percent of children raised in Adventist homes leave the faith of their parents at some point. Sadder still, most never return.

I do not claim to possess any secret formula or magic tricks to convert all of our youth. If I did, I could bottle the recipe, and every Christian mother and father would pay a king's ransom to purchase it. I also do not think there is any one list of steps we can take guaranteed to save all our children. I have seen Christian families, complete with a loving father and mother, whose children have grown up, some still in the church, some out of the church, and some wobbling on the fence.

Remember that Adam and Eve had one Cain and one Abel and other sons and daughters. There may not be a secret recipe, but I do believe there are some things we can do to vastly improve our children's chances for conversion and salvation.

The thoughts I am sharing are based on the Bible, personal observations, and experience. As a father of four, I know something of the joys and sorrows of watching, working, and praying for my own children's salvation. There have been many times when I have even had to pray that the Lord would overrule or reverse my bad decisions and poor influence.

Parents and teachers, please remember that it will never help to waste time wallowing in regret for your past mistakes. In some cases, though, it would be a very good idea if we approached the young people we have wronged by our words or example and honestly apologized to them.

There is no greater human love than that of parents for a child. Being a parent teaches us more about God's love for us than does any other human experience. The Bible says Enoch lived for sixty-five years and then had Methuselah (Genesis 5:21). After having a child, he better understood the infinite love of our heavenly Father. Then Enoch walked with God for three hundred years.

King David had a rebellious son named Absalom. He was killed in a battle to usurp his father's kingdom. When David learned the tragic truth that his ungrateful son was dead, the king wept and lamented for hours. "O my son Absalom—my son, my son Absalom—if only I had died in your place! O Absalom, my son, my son!" (2 Samuel 18:33).

Do you hear the undying love of a human father for his erring, wayward child? How much more does our heavenly Father love His sinful children in that He would willingly offer His Son to save them?

As we approach the ways young people can survive in church, remember that God loves our children infinitely more than any earthly parent and is desperate to have them saved.

How young people can survive
Problem: "Adults never listen."

Solution: Listen better. The teenage years are often a most insecure time for young people. They need lots of attention during this time. One reason they always seem to try to shock their parents is to find out if they're listening. They strive for attention—even if it's negative attention.

Problem: "Most Christians are hypocrites. They say one thing and live another."

Solution: Be a good example. This is easier said than done! If church attendance and Sabbath keeping are not important to you, they will not be important to your children. If you think an occasional glass of wine is all right, then don't be alarmed when your children want an occasional puff of pot or snort of cocaine. They will value what you value. If your Christian witness is inconsistent, your children will be the first to know.

One of the most positive things that can happen is for your children to see you on your knees in personal devotions and for them to know that Jesus is your personal friend. Albert Schweitzer said there are three ways to teach children: "First, example. Second, example. Third, example!"

Problem: "There's nothing for me at church."

Solution: Talk to the pastor and Sabbath School leaders to see what they are doing for the youth. Ask your pastor if he will incorporate the youth into the services at least once a quarter or more. If your church is like many other churches, this complaint may be legitimate. However, it does not have to stay that way.

We need to find more ways to involve our younger members in all phases of ministry and stop giving them the message that they don't count. When the church holds a church business meeting or Sabbath School Council meeting, ask your leader how our younger members can be included. Too often, the youth are shuffled off to play games while the "real members" settle all the problems and plan all the programs. The youth may just surprise you with the ideas they can contribute if given the opportunity.

Problem: "My parents make me go to church."

Solution: Our attitude can make a big difference. Don't tell them they *have* to go to church; tell them they *get* to go! Make Sabbath and church a very special time. Talk about it all week. Have special clothes to wear, and plan special events for the afternoon. Invite another family over for lunch and a nature outing. Become your child's advocate to see that your church values youth, ministers to their needs, and gives them opportunities for service. In this way, they will become so involved, they won't want to stop attending church when it's time to leave home.

Even if they attend church reluctantly for a while, at least they are exposed to the right influences of the gospel. They will be in an environment to learn about Christ and to make a decision for Him. We don't want our children to feel "forced" to go to church, but at the same time, we cannot, as responsible parents, let them stay home because they are not in the mood to attend.

Also remember that the commandment in Exodus 20:10 states:

> The seventh day is the Sabbath of the Lord your God. In it you shall do no work: you, nor your son, nor your daughter, nor your [male servant], nor your [female servant], nor your cattle, nor your stranger who is within your gates.

Like the little boy forced to sit in a chair who remarked to his mother, "My body may be sitting down, but inside I'm standing up," forced church attendance cannot win the soul of your youngster. Pray continually for your child. As parents, we are responsible for what our children do while they are within our gates (our homes), and Sabbath observance includes church attendance.

Problem: "I don't understand why church attendance is so important."

Solution: Our young people need to be converted. This is really the key, perhaps the only issue, when it comes to young people surviving in church. They must see the importance and urgency of their own need for salvation from sin.

We must not fail to show God's love to our teens, or they will fail to see the gospel at work in our lives. Adult members need to be "Christianity, with skin on it" to children who cannot feel the love of God through a sermon but can see it modeled in our lives.

In essence, you cannot expect your children to rise spiritually any higher than the example you set. Church will become a priority for your children even through the teen years, when they see the change in your life and sense their own need of a Saviour. When we gloss over sin or speak lightly of God's Word or critically of the pastor and members, our young people get the message that none of this really counts anyway, so church becomes frivolous.

Let your children hear you praying for them by name during the week. Involve your children in family worship at home, where they can discover the relevance of God's Word for daily living. You are having family worship, aren't you? Share with them your answers to prayer, and encourage them to have a prayer life of their own.

The teen years may be rough ones as our youth strive to show their budding independence. They can survive. They can make it through their teens and into early adulthood and still be in the church. Hopefully, their faith will increase with age, until they become part of that next group of members in our church—namely, the singles.

Chapter 9

Surviving as a Single in Church

He that is unmarried careth for the things that belong to the Lord, how he may please the Lord (1 Corinthians 7:32, KJV).

You know singles need help surviving in church when:

> . . . eligible male visitors are welcomed with wreaths of flowers.

> . . . more single moms accompany their boys to the father-son picnic than dads.

> . . . the largest Sabbath School class is called "Widows and the Word."

> . . . the pastor has not conducted a wedding in two years.

Kay joined the church when she was twenty-one and single. The congregation in Driftwood was small, but they made up for it by being friendly. Because Kay was the only member between the ages of twelve and thirty, she sometimes felt isolated. The loneliness was especially acute at church outings and potlucks. Those programs always seemed "family" oriented and made Kay feel like a penguin in a pond of ducks.

The Smiths did have a college-age son, Ted, who came home to Driftwood on school breaks, and everyone soon began to speculate as to when the sparks of love would ignite. The only problem was that no one bothered to ask Kay or Ted if they were even interested in each other. They weren't. Even though Kay felt a little out of place in the Driftwood Church, she did not want to rush into marriage just so she could "fit in."

The older folks in the church encouraged Kay to go to one of our Adventist colleges. Naturally, the members secretly hoped that Kay would meet a nice, young, eligible, Adventist Christian man and get married.

Kay arrived on campus and began making friends with the other young women in the dormitory. They were full of advice for this newcomer to an Adventist campus and told her, "The guys you have to watch out for are the ones taking pastoral training. They have trouble getting a job as pastors unless they are married, so they are desperate."

"Don't worry, I'm not interested in dating or marriage right now," she told them. "I just want to finish my education and get started with a career."

But, sure enough, the first weekend of school, Kay went to a Sabbath-afternoon Bible-study group and got cornered by a nice theology student named Stanley. She didn't want to be rude, but she had to keep trying to avoid him until the sun finally went down and she had a good excuse to leave, saying she needed to do homework. Kay realized being single had its blessings and challenges.

If you are from the growing section of our church that is single, you can probably sympathize a little with Kay's experience.

There are two categories of survival help for the single. First, what the church can do to help singles. Second, what singles can do to help themselves.

What the church can do

1. Be inclusive. Find ways to include the singles. Don't give them the message "We'll let you participate as soon as you are married and live like 'normal' people." Show that you value your singles as people. Include them as resources in all phases of church ministry.

2. Be considerate of their needs. Some singles, such as single parents, have special needs. Try asking them if they need someone to sit with their children during church to allow them to fill some other function (such as being a greeter or a deacon) or just allow them a break. This applies to time during the week as well. Single parents need an opportunity to have some time by themselves. Offering to baby-sit for a few hours can be a tremendous help to them.

Recently divorced or widowed persons have a variety of special needs. They need time to grieve the loss of their spouse as well as help doing the practical chores the missing mate had been doing. A home-cooked meal is always welcomed on Sabbath or any other day of the week. Some may need help straightening out their finances, repairing the car or the house roof, etc. The church should be there to help fill the painful vacuum that is left when people lose a mate by divorce or death.

3. Become family to the single. Holidays can be especially lonely for the single person. The church can often fill the role of family to the singles during this stressful time. Have you ever thought of adopting a single person at your church for the holidays? But don't just stop there. Holidays aren't the only lonely times they face. Every Sabbath can seem like a solitary Christmas to the single person.

From time to time, don't forget to give the single a brotherly or sisterly hug. You know, the generic kind. Truly, people need a human touch.

4. Respect their privacy. The matter of a single's private life should not be the subject of gossip, rumor, or interrogation. A person's life is not open for inspection just because he or she has never married. The same is true with divorced or widowed persons. Not everyone needs to know the circumstances of a divorce or how the surviving spouse is dealing with his or her loss.

Likewise, allow singles to make their own plans and decisions about marriage rather than suffer being objects of a church plot to "matchmake."

What single people can do

1. Live in the present. The Bible says, "Do not worry about tomorrow, for tomorrow will worry about its own things" (Matthew 6:34).

We usually apply this text to not worrying about things, and so we should. But it also means not to be constantly looking to the future or the past before you start living.

Singles looking toward marriage need not put off living today. Just because you aren't married doesn't mean you can't have nice furniture or you have to eat from paper plates. Go ahead and fix a whole meal rather than just grabbing something out of the refrigerator!

On the other hand, divorced or widowed singles need to let the past be the past. Things will never be the same as they once were, but that doesn't mean they have to be worse. A loving spouse certainly wouldn't want his death to completely prevent his widow from going on. He would be happy to know his mate not only survived, but succeeded.

The victim of a divorce also needs to let go of the past, but for the opposite reason. To let divorce keep you living in the past and never going on is to let painful memories or bitterness control your present. To pick up and go on and succeed are the best ways to heal when you have been through this painful process.

2. Develop your talents. Whether you are looking toward marriage or not, you have been given talents by God for which you are held accountable. Being single is no excuse for letting your talents rust and atrophy. Go ahead and work toward improving them by continuing your education. Being single may actually give you more time and opportunity to do this.

3. Develop a support network. Singles especially need a network of supportive friends and counselors. Most singles are separated from their families and spend much of their time alone. Seek out friends and godly advisors from your church family. If your congregation is too small for this, join one of the many church-affiliated singles' ministries. Just knowing you are not alone can be a big help. If your church doesn't have a singles' ministry, start one.

There is a temptation to find friends only interested in secular things or to spend your time in temporal pursuits. The most important thing is that your support network be such that it contributes to your spiritual health rather than detracting from it.

4. Keep your eye single. Though it may be difficult to be single if you would rather be married, don't let this desire ruin your life by letting it take your focus off Christ. Marriage is not the solution to living the abundant life; Jesus is. Remember, as boring as it may seem today, the single life is much more fulfilling than a bad marriage.

Many singles have a tendency to fantasize about marriage or about having a family. They think, "If only I were married, I wouldn't have to spend all my time alone." This may sound true, but it doesn't take into account that many married people spend the majority of their time apart or, worse yet, together arguing. Parents with small children would tell you they envy the time you have to yourself as a single. Not having a family can also mean not having those family feuds. If the grass looks greener on the other side of the fence, it's probably just taller and needs more mowing.

Some singles also make the mistake of taking their eyes off Christ and looking for a spouse outside their faith. They think any spouse would be better than remaining single. Ask almost anyone who has made this mistake, and they will tell you how much they regret their decision. It is better to stay single forever than to face thirty or forty years in a divided marriage.

5. Take advantage of your advantage. Being single is not necessarily a handicap. We sometimes forget that when our Lord and Saviour, Jesus Christ, walked on this earth, He was single. The apostle Paul has some interesting words about being single. He desired that everyone would feel the way he did, for the single can offer undivided service to God.

Paul writes in 1 Corinthians 7:32-34:

I would have you to be without care. He who is unmarried cares for the things that belong to the Lord—

how he may please the Lord. But he who is married cares about the things of the world—how he may please his wife. There is difference between a wife and a virgin. The unmarried woman cares about the things of the Lord, that she may be holy both in body and in spirit. But she who is married cares about the things of the world—how she may please her husband.

Remember, finding and choosing a lifelong mate is serious business and is God's business. Leave it in the hands of the Lord to work out your life in His way and in His time. Isaac didn't marry until he was forty years of age; then God found the perfect mate for him.

6. Avoid sexual quicksand. Any single person with a fully operational body will understand this danger zone. When dating, be careful to avoid situations that are calculated to get out of hand. Becoming involved in heavy petting and kissing will set into operation a biological process you cannot easily reverse! Keep your mind out of the forbidden zone. The greatest part of sexual stimulation is in the brain. With God's help, you can keep your mind pure and avoid unnecessary frustration.

To sum it up, being single is not a curse. Making a bad choice by marrying too quickly or marrying outside the faith can make the cure worse than the disease! You can survive by taking advantage of the availability the single life offers you to become involved in ministry as part of the church family.

Your commitment to Christ needs to come first. A life that is full because Christ makes you whole will be a witness to your church family and to the world. However, putting Christ on the back burner while you try to look for a mate will just leave you burned.

Paul puts it even stronger when he writes to Timothy about young widows or anyone else eager to get married:

Don't put the younger widows on your list. My experience is that when their natural desires grow stronger than their spiritual devotion to Christ they want to marry again, thus proving themselves unfaithful to their first loyalty (1 Timothy 5:11, 12, Phillips, Revised Edition).

Though Paul does advise young widows to marry so that the church will not be brought into scandal by their wandering, he doesn't see marriage as the ultimate way to serve God. He merely saw marriage at that time as a way to provide financially for women.

He writes:

My advice is that the younger widows should, normally, marry again, bear children and run their own households. They should certainly not be the means of lowering the reputation of the Church, although some, alas, have already played into the enemy's hands (1 Timothy 5:14, Phillips).

I think it would be safe to say that Paul would have approved of women staying single if there had been a way for their financial needs to be met and a way for them to serve the Lord. Actually, that is what he recommended for the older widows.

The important thing is that people's desire for a mate not overshadow their love for Christ, or they could be prone to a scandal. In the next chapter, the people of Shockingtown find out about that.

Chapter 10

Surviving Scandal

David sent and inquired about the woman. And someone said, "Is this not Bathsheba, the daughter of Eliam, the wife of Uriah the Hittite?" (2 Samuel 11:3).

You know your church is in trouble when:

> . . . the pastor's picture appears on the cover of the *National Enquirer*.

> . . . the church treasurer is arrested for shoplifting.

> . . . the choir loft doubles as the press box.

> . . . the benediction invites you to tune in for next week's episode.

Pastor Al Dultry, of the Shockingtown SDA Church, appeared to have his life all together. He was a sensitive, organized, and able teacher. Under his dynamic leadership, the church attendance had nearly doubled in two years. Because of their community involvement, the church's reputation had vastly improved among the citizens of Shockingtown. Then it happened.

As the people came into the church one Sabbath morning, the foyer was humming with conversation. People's mouths dropped open. Some were sitting in the sanctuary sobbing, while others, after hearing the tragic story, simply turned around and walked out of the church with anguish on their faces! As the sad details came together, it left everyone feeling numb.

Evidently, for over a year, Pastor Al Dultry had been having a secret affair. What's worse, it was with the church youth leader. And worse still, the youth leader was a man! They had run off together to Glitter City, leaving their wives, children, and a paralyzed church behind.

For several weeks after the scandal was known, church attendance was way down. In the middle of her Sabbath School talk, the superintendent broke into tears and hurried to the restroom. It was mainly the "older" members who held things together. They had weathered so many other storms; they knew "this too shall pass." The newer members and the younger families were especially devastated.

"We thought the Holy Spirit was speaking through Pastor Al. Were we wrong?" they asked. Since everyone in Shockingtown had heard what happened, they were embarrassed to attend this church.

But God's church has been surviving scandal for ages. From the time Cain killed his brother to David's adultery with Bathsheba to Peter's denial of Jesus, Satan has been seeking to dishearten God's children by the scandalous behavior of some. The devil knows that when he can successfully tempt some Christians to misbehave, it will cause many to turn away from the church.

So how does a church survive a devastating scandal such as this? Time. Yes, *time* is the key word. Time is a wonderful healer. As time goes by, people's minds become occupied with other things. Today's headlines will be tomorrow's historical footnotes.

Faithful Christians must not allow the hypocrites in the church to control their experience. Many churches fail to recover from internal scandal because they don't deal with the party who brought reproach on the name of the Lord.

By this, I mean that if church members openly shame Jesus and His cause, they should be removed from the church. By doing this, the church makes a statement to other members, as well as to the community, that they do not approve of this behavior and that their standards mean something. If we don't stand for something, we will certainly fall for anything!

Someone will always argue, "We must love them through this sinful experience." Right! But love does not mean letting them continue on their destructive course with church approval.

This is just what Matthew 18:17 means: "If he refuses to hear them [the counsel of a few witnesses], tell it unto the church. But if he refuses even to hear the church, let him be to you like a heathen and a tax collector."

The heathen man and the publican are the mission fields of the church and the object of its loving call to the Saviour. By disfellowshiping the person involved in open sin, the church demonstrates that they love that person enough to consider him as someone whose soul they need to win back to the Lord. Dropping his name from the church membership roll really is the best way to show our love. If we didn't care, we would just ignore him and leave him where he is and allow him to remain in his lost condition. This not only hurts the person involved in open sin, by not warning him of his perilous state, but it devitalizes the church by subtly telling everyone they can commit the same sin and not have any consequences.

The open sinner knows he's doing wrong, and inaction by the church lets him think he's getting away with it. This may make the sinner feel better temporarily, but it is deadly for the church.

Just as Israel fell to the enemy when they allowed Achan to get away with sin, there are consequences to the church that indulges sin (see Joshua 7). The reason many churches are constantly defeated in spiritual battles is because they have so many Achans in the camp. They couldn't win a war if they had nuclear weapons!

The decision to remove a name from the church books does *not* mean that that person should be shunned or alienated from the church family. The church should continue to reach out, leading and loving this person back to Christ.

But being a member of God's church is a special honor and privilege. Because of this, we need to uphold His standards.

The church that refuses to discipline a rebellious member is standing in the way of God's dealing with that person. For example, Jonah knew he was running from God. He even told the sailors to throw him overboard. But at first they were too much like the modern church. They said in effect, "But, Jonah, that's not very loving. We would rather have the whole ship go down in this tempest than to throw you overboard."

Instead of having to deal with just one rebellious person, now God had a whole shipload of them. So, the storm kept getting worse until the sailors threw Jonah overboard. Then they had smooth sailing. Likewise, entire congregations may face God's discipline because they tolerate one Jonah or Achan.

Another way to survive scandal is to remember not to allow someone else's failure to be your failure. As a Christian, you must follow Jesus. He *never* fails. Don't focus on people. As a Christian, you should live a life that people can look at, but you must not look at other people as your examples.

> Each man should examine his own conduct for himself; then he can measure his achievement by comparing himself with himself and not with anyone else (Galatians 6:4, NEB).

> Even if a man should be detected in some sin, my brothers, the spiritual ones among you should quietly set him back on the right path, not with any feeling of superiority but being yourselves on guard against temptation (Galatians 6:1, Phillips, Revised Edition).

It is a good idea to spend time on your knees before you confront anyone. Ask the Lord to forgive you of your own sins and to give you His heart of love.

To those who are eager to "call sin by its right name" in others without looking at their own sins, Jesus warns:

> Why do you look at the speck of sawdust in your brother's eye, with never a thought for the great plank in your own? . . . You hypocrite! First take the plank out of your own eye, and then you will see clearly to take the

speck out of your brother's (Matthew 7:3-5, NEB).

Scandals can be survived, with time, if they are dealt with in a Christ-like manner. Discipline may be needed. If the discipline is given with a loving and redemptive attitude, the wrongdoer can be pointed back to where the focus needs to be—on Jesus.

When the focus is taken off Christ, scandal in the church becomes the fuel for gossip.

Chapter 11

Surviving Gossip

If anyone does not stumble in word, he is a perfect man, able also to bridle the whole body (James 3:2).

You know you are in a gossip-filled church when:

> . . . everyone's favorite hymn is "I Love to Tell the Story."

> . . . the pastor threatens to record all phone conversations.

> . . . the Dorcas women specialize in secondhand rumors.

> . . . the church has never successfully had a surprise party.

A fine Seventh-day Adventist pastor and his family moved to a small town to take up their new work in the church. As they were unpacking, church members and well-wishing neighbors came to offer help and drop off some housewarming gifts.

The neighbors next door owned a local grocery store, so they thought it would be nice to welcome their new neighbors with a few bags of grocery items—some staples like flour, sugar, bacon, potatoes, hamburger, coffee, and a bottle of wine to celebrate their new home. Being good Catholics, they figured this Adventist "priest" would eat and drink like their parish father.

The pastor and his wife graciously thanked the grocer and his family for their kindness, without even glancing to see what was in the bags of groceries. A little while after their neighbors left, the pastor and his wife began to take things out of the bags and place them on the kitchen table. They laughed and rolled their eyes as they saw some of the "forbidden" contents. They decided to tactfully return the items they could not use the next day. And with that, they continued unpacking.

Then wouldn't you know, Sister Gabriella Gossip from the church came to offer her services, which consisted of updating the new pastor on all the members—their strengths and faults. Mostly faults. While Sister Gabriella was educating the pastor on the finer points of human nature with all of its weaknesses, the pastor continued unpacking with an occasional, "Uh-huh, I see."

The sister happened to glance off into the kitchen and saw all these "questionable" grocery items on the table—coffee, wine, and bacon. Suddenly, she told the pastor she had to leave. She had just remembered there was someone else she needed to visit.

Before the sun went down that day, Sister Gabby had told all the members of the church that the new pastor didn't believe the Bible, he ate unclean food, and he was an alcoholic.

When the first Sabbath came and the pastor stood up to speak, he couldn't understand why the members seemed so cold and withdrawn. Soon these untrue rumors spread to the community, and by the time some of the people discovered the source of this misunderstanding, the damage was irreversible. After a few months of unfruitful ministry, the pastor and his family thought it best to move on.

All this damage was from spreading rumors and gossip. This story is based on a true account. You may think it could never happen to you, but it could!

> Even so the tongue is a little member, and boasts great things. See, how great a forest a little fire kindles! (James 3:5).

A church member told me, "I don't gossip. Everything I say

is true." Perhaps we should differentiate between gossip and constructive information. Webster's definition for *gossip* is "to chatter idly about others." True or false, it's gossip. Jesus tells us, "every *idle* word that men shall speak, they shall give account thereof in the day of judgment" (Matthew 12:36, emphasis supplied).

I read that magnetic storms can sometimes play tricks on phone lines and transfer conversations to radio frequencies. A few years back, one such storm in New York transferred a very private and intimate conversation to a coast-to-coast radio program.

In our little Covelo church, the P.A. system had the tendency to pick up radio transmissions from local police and ambulance drivers. For the record, I will have you know that our public servants do not always use the "king's English." During the worship service, we would hear things that should not be part of any sermon. If only those people knew that their vulgar bantering was being broadcast in a local church, what a difference it would have made in their speech! And if only we would remember that angels and God are hearing everything we say, it would season our words with grace.

Ellen White writes:

> If all these gossipers would ever bear in mind that an angel is following them, recording their words, there would be less talking and much more praying (*Testimonies for the Church*, 4:40).

Usually, the people who gossip the most don't feel good about themselves, so they find relief in talking about the faults of others. Those who throw the most mud usually have the dirtiest hands, and I'm sure you know that the fastest way to make a mountain out of a molehill is to add a little dirt.

When we talk about surviving gossip, we need to consider it from three sides: the gossiper, the listener, and the one talked about.

The gossiper

Don't say anything about anyone that is not kind or constructive. Remember the golden rule, "Do unto others what you would want them to do unto you." Or you might put it this way: "Say" about others what you would want them to "say" about you!

In the Living Bible, Proverbs 10:19 says: "Don't talk so much. You keep putting your foot in your mouth. Be sensible and turn off the flow!"

Everyone likes to hear juicy news. That's why the number-one-selling papers in the U.S. are the supermarket tabloids. Nobody respects these newspapers, even though millions of Americans buy them. Likewise, no one respects gossipers, even though everyone listens to them. People will listen to you if you gossip, but they will not respect you. They know that when they're not around, you are probably talking about them too!

I read somewhere that "great minds talk about the future. Average minds talk about current events. Feeble minds talk about people."

All Christians should speak in such a way that they would not be afraid to sell the family parrot to the church gossip.

The listener

Don't be a listener. When someone launches into a slimy story about someone else, refuse to listen, or change the subject. This makes gossipers ashamed and discourages this behavior. Don't participate in gossiping by listening. God judges us as if we were the blabbers ourselves.

I once lived in a small town where a good Christian woman worked as the postmaster at the local post office. As people came in and out each day, they would always try to engage Mary Brown in the juicy local news. But being a good Christian lady, she would simply smile and go on working and would never give any response or reaction to this kind of "news." When someone would speak unkindly about another person, she pretended that she didn't even hear it. Everyone in town respected her as a good Christian because she could not be enticed to engage in any of the local gossip.

The victim (or the one talked about)

What do you do if you discover that you are the victim of vicious gossip? Well, first, you must ask yourself if it's true. You may have brought it on yourself by some scandalous behavior. If you ran down Main Street stark naked and drunk, then you can't really pretend you are surprised and outraged when people talk about it.

Now, remember, this is still no excuse for Christians to gossip or listen, but we know that many in the church are not converted and that gossiping is the norm for those with carnal hearts. So, if you behaved in a way you are ashamed of, you may need to do some apologizing—privately—to individuals, if it was a private matter, or publicly, if you sinned publicly.

But what if you are a victim of untrue or grossly exaggerated gossip?

Remember Jesus. He was probably the most talked about Man in His day. He was accused of being illegitimate, a glutton, a drunkard, and an agent of the devil. How did our Lord respond to all these false charges? He usually ignored the ridiculous accusations and lived and worked in such a way that no one would listen to such nonsense. If someone throws mud at you, it will look much worse if you try to wipe it off. Just keep living in the sunshine, and it will dry and fall off without a stain.

Nehemiah is another example of someone who was the victim of a smear campaign. Sanballat and his cohorts tried to use a gossiping letter to deter Nehemiah from doing the Lord's work. Nehemiah didn't even give them the time of day. He just persisted in doing what the Lord wanted him to do. He answered his detractors with:

> I *am* doing a great work, so that I cannot come down. Why should the work cease, while I leave it and go down to you? (Nehemiah 6:3).

We can follow Nehemiah's example of not allowing gossip to sidetrack us. When you think about it, Nehemiah's answer was pretty accurate. Giving in to gossip makes you "come down" to the level of your gossipers. But living the way Jesus wants you to will lift you up.

There is one kind of gossip that is probably more damaging in our churches than idle chatter about people and their shocking behavior. That is gossip about God's Word. This is what I would call "tabloid theology." Tabloid theology is that line of rumors and debate about church leaders and God's word that brings confusion and division. Perhaps it has already come to your church and found you vulnerable, and you are left with those lingering questions.

Our next chapter tells you how to survive doctrinal doubts.

Chapter 12

Surviving Doctrinal Doubts

There is going to come a time when people won't listen to the truth, but will go around looking for teachers who will tell them just what they want to hear. They won't listen to what the Bible says but will blithely follow their own misguided ideas (2 Timothy 4:3, 4, TLB).

You know your church is doctrinally confused when:

> . . . they think the epistles are the wives of the apostles.

> . . . they think the forbidden fruit Adam and Eve ate was an apple.

> . . . they think the millennium is a lottery prize.

"Dorothy, you have nearly finished this set of Bible studies. Have you given any thought to being baptized and joining our church?" Cathy asked.

"Oh, Cathy," Dorothy answered, "I have really enjoyed studying with you, and I am convinced of all the truths you have been sharing with me, but I could never join your church."

"Why not?" Cathy queried.

"Well, it's just that red is my favorite color, and I don't know that I could give up wearing it," Dorothy confessed.

As Cathy questioned Dorothy further, she discovered that

Dorothy had visited the Hob Knob Church one Sabbath and listened to the pastor's sermon with interest.

"When the pastor said 'wearing red is a sin,' I knew I could never join this church. I just looked down with shame at my red shoes," Dorothy sobbed.

Cathy ended her study with Dorothy and hurried off to visit the pastor.

"Just what did you tell Dorothy?" she demanded of the pastor.

The pastor looked confused as Cathy related Dorothy's story. Then the lights went on.

"She must be thinking of my sermon on temptation," he began. "I was trying to give an illustration of how women who dress seductively are enticing men to sin. I said that the woman who wore a slinky red dress to attract attention was just as guilty as the man who lusted after her," the pastor explained. "She must have misunderstood my illustration."

Cathy was only too happy to be able to share this with Dorothy the next time they met. "I don't know where you ever got the idea that not wearing red was one of our doctrines," she told Dorothy.

"What a relief," Dorothy sighed. "I really do want to be a part of your church family. I'm so glad my red shoes won't keep me out."

It would be nice if all doctrinal doubts could be as easily solved as Dorothy's battle over the red shoes, but sadly, this is not the case.

As we approach the end of time, Satan will intensify his efforts to confuse and obscure the line of truth. There's a sanctifying power in the truth.

John 17:17 says, "Sanctify them by Your truth. Your word is truth." It is a power that frees us. John 8:32 adds, "You shall know the truth, and the truth shall make you free."

All doctrinal truth works, to some degree, as a safeguard against sin. Satan tries to loosen the guardrail of truth so we'll dive off the precipice into ruin. The devil will see to it that there always will be hooks on which we can hang our doubts.

Only God knows all. But at the same time, Jesus will see to it that we have abundant evidence on which to hang our faith.

It is so important to understand truth. Jesus said: "I am . . . the truth" (John 14:6).

Any rejection of truth, in any measure, is in some way a rejection of Christ. That's why it is so important to know the truth. Knowing the truth is related to our knowing the Lord.

Five steps to survive or remove doctrinal doubts

1. Study more. "Be diligent to present yourself approved to God, a worker who does not need to be ashamed, rightly dividing the word of truth" (2 Timothy 2:15).

Many are confused as to what is true, because they listen to the reasoning of human beings instead of the Word of God. "But I don't understand this subject," they say. Well, then seek, knock, and ask with all your heart (Matthew 7:7, 8; Jeremiah 29:13).

Every effort to better understand the truth is, in reality, an effort to know Jesus better. And He's worth it. If any of us lack wisdom, the Bible says: "Let him ask of God, who gives to all [people] liberally" (James 1:5).

2. Play it safe. When you are in doubt about a subject of truth or some doctrine, take the "safe" position until you are sure of the facts.

For example, suppose you are not sure if a Christian should drink any alcoholic beverage. I have heard many clever arguments in favor of drinking a moderate amount of wine, some even trying to use Scripture. But until you are certain of God's will in this matter, play it "safe." Don't drink any alcoholic beverages.

Picture with me the judgment day. God will not exclude anyone from heaven because they did not drink enough alcohol or because they did not wear enough jewelry. No one will be kept out of heaven because they kept the Sabbath too carefully. So play it "safe."

The problem with human nature is that we want to see how close to the world we can get—how close to the edge we can be without falling off. We want to enjoy as many questionable pleasures as possible and still slide through the pearly gates by the skin of our teeth.

Many ask the question, "What's wrong with it?" We should be asking, "What's right with it?" Or we ask, "Is a little OK?" We know very well that none would be better.

I had friends who tried to see how far they could lean while riding a motorcycle on a turn before they would reach that critical point and crash. It seems this is what some people are doing with the Christian experience. They want to see how very close to sin they can lean until they, too, reach that critical point and fall.

3. Ask, "What would Jesus do?" This is always the best approach to solving any question. However, sometimes it is the most challenging. Jesus was radically different and revolutionary from the popular Jewish traditions in His teachings. A Christian is a follower of Christ, not of a church. Sometimes we may find that the teachings of Jesus are different from the teachings of the "traditional" norm.

Is it OK for a Christian to go to movies? Ask, "What would Jesus do?"

Should a Christian play the lottery? Ask, "What would Jesus do?"

Is it OK to read this book? Well, would you feel comfortable reading it to Jesus?

Thousands of doubts and questions could be settled instantly by applying this simple litmus test—"What would Jesus do?" If you don't know the answer, it could be because you don't know the Lord. So get to know Him better!

4. Be willing to do His will. God's Word promises: "If anyone wants to do his will, he shall know concerning the doctrine, whether it is from God" (John 7:17).

In reality, the reason for many doctrinal doubts is not that we don't understand but that we don't want to understand! *A pretense of confusion is sometimes a cloak to cover an unwilling or unconverted heart.*

In order to arrive at truth, we must have a sincere desire to know the truth and a willingness of heart to obey it (*Steps to Christ*, 111).

Often, at an evangelistic meeting, when I present the Sabbath truth, one of the listeners will approach me and say, "I don't understand this subject." After talking with them awhile, I will discover that they could lose their job if they accepted the Sabbath truth. In reality, they don't think they can afford to understand the requirements of the Sabbath! It's a lack of willingness. As the saying goes, "It's not the parts I don't understand that I have a problem with, it's the parts I do understand."

The greatest battle that Jesus fought for us was in the Garden of Gethsemane when He prayed, "Not my will, but Thy will be done." If we in sincerity pray that prayer from our hearts, then God becomes responsible for making His will known to us. One of the most important things to do in understanding truth is to be willing to follow truth.

Ellen White puts it like this:

If you will seek the Lord and be converted every day; if you will of your own spiritual choice be free and joyous in God; if with gladsome consent of heart to His gracious call you come wearing the yoke of Christ,—the yoke of obedience and service,—all your murmurings will be stilled, all your difficulties will be removed, all the perplexing problems that now confront you will be solved (*Thoughts From the Mount of Blessing*, 101).

5. Be faithful to what you do know. There will always be room for doubt, but we don't need to focus on this doubt! The Bible has enough plainly revealed truth to keep us busy while we allow time for deciphering the difficult.

Acts 19:2-6 tells the story of some people who followed this guideline. They were busy rejoicing in their faith, never even knowing that Christ had come or that there was a Holy Spirit. When Paul enlightened them about these facts, they were only too happy to be rebaptized. Then the Lord blessed them by giving them the Holy Spirit. My point is this: they may not have known everything, but they were faithful to what they did know.

I know too many people who have let doctrinal doubts turn them bitter. Instead of waiting on the Lord and seeking His will, they have focused on their doubts and spread them to others like a contagious disease. Too often, even honest questions have turned vicious, and people's feelings have been hurt. There's no reason to let hurt or disappointment keep you out of the kingdom. It is possible to survive this as well.

Chapter 13

Surviving Hurt and Disappointment

The Lord doth build up Jerusalem: he gathereth together the outcasts of Israel. He healeth the broken in heart, and bindeth up their wounds (Psalm 147:2, 3, KJV).

You know the church has hurt you when:

> . . . you are only asked to do special music for the church-board meetings.

> . . . they send you a get-well card for your birthday.

> . . . the only people who ever greet you Sabbath mornings are the visitors.

Sam tried not to blame God when Becky left, but he felt he had a right to be angry. Two years into what appeared to be a happy marriage, little Tyler was born. Sam was elated to be a father and have a son, but soon after the birth, Becky began to act strange and sullen.

Then one day, upon returning home from work, Sam noticed the other car was gone. Becky's things were cleared out of the bedroom, and little six-month-old Tyler was sitting in his crib, crying, with a note taped to the headboard. Becky had quickly scratched on a single piece of paper, "I don't want to be married anymore, and I don't want to be a mother. Just leave me alone."

It was several days before he began to recover from the shock

and could even function. When Sam turned to their pastor for help, the pastor kept assuming Sam must have done something terrible to make a nice young woman like Becky just up and leave. In the weeks that followed, Sam continued to attend church services but refused to ask any church members for help. He had to learn to be a father and mother to little Tyler, leaving him with a baby sitter during the day, then coming home after work to cook, clean, and care for his son.

Then one Sabbath during the worship service, little Tyler was squirming and fussing more than ever. Sam tried to quiet his restless child, but to no avail. Suddenly the woman in the pew behind him snapped, "If you can't control your brat, at least you could take him out so we can hear the service!" That was it. Sam scooped up Tyler and, in a rage, marched out the door. He did not return for twenty-one years.

Sad story, I know, but this is just the kind of disappointing experience that many people use for an excuse to leave the church—for years, or even forever! Some pain is relived over and over in memory's halls until it is etched there permanently, like a wound that never heals. Why does this happen?

> Is there no balm in Gilled, is there no physician there? Why then is there no recovery for the health of the daughter of my people? (Jeremiah 8:22).

The Lord, too, wonders why we let those hurts and disappointments, little or big, keep us from church and fellowship.

The psalmist wrote: "Great peace have these who love Your law: and nothing causes them to stumble" (Psalm 119:165). Oh, that we all were filled with this peace! The saying goes, "Sticks and stones may break my bones, but words can never hurt me." Yet, the church is full of people who have been hurt by words. If you were to ask these people, many of them would have preferred the sticks and stones, because physical wounds heal more quickly.

Jesus, too, suffered taunts and abuse from His own people. They even crucified Him. Zechariah prophesied of Christ:

> Someone will say to him, "What are these wounds in your hands?" Then he will answer, "Those with which I was wounded in the house of my friends" (Zechariah 13:6).

Today, we might say, "That's where my friends stuck it to me." Remember, in all your suffering, He knows. He understands, He's been there before. However, just knowing you have One who sympathizes with you isn't enough. You need to know how to survive, how to get over your hurts and disappointments, how to let those wounds heal.

How to let your wounds heal

1. Pray for those you resent. Stacy felt she had been treated unfairly at work. Every year, a team from her workplace went on a wonderful retreat. The first year, Stacy wasn't selected because she had only been there a short time. The resentment began when she was passed by the next year and a brand-new worker was selected to go. Stacy realized that her resentment for the new worker was getting in the way of her doing her work, but she didn't know what to do.

Finally, Stacy asked her supervisor how to handle this feeling of resentment. Stacy didn't really expect him to understand, because as far as she knew, he wasn't a Christian. So his answer surprised her.

He told her, "Well, this is what I do when I discover I have a resentment. For the next two weeks, I pray for that person every day and ask God to bless her with all the blessings I would want for myself. I ask Him to give her just the blessing that would make her happiest. After I do that, my resentment just melts away, and I actually look forward to God blessing the person I once resented."

The supervisor's answer left Stacy with nothing more to say, but with a lot of praying to do. Stacy was ashamed of herself for holding onto those resentments. She felt bad that someone who she didn't even know believed in God had to tell her that by giving her resentment to God in prayer, she would find her answer.

Job 42:10 is a promise for anyone who has been wounded or has resentments toward others. It reads:

> The Lord restored Job's losses when he prayed for his friends. Indeed the Lord gave Job twice as much as he had before.

The "twice as much" the Lord promises is not always material things like He gave Job, but it is often the spiritual blessing of seeing the Lord bless the person for whom we are praying and knowing that it is our prayer the Lord is answering. Both you and the person you resented can win from this kind of prayer!

2. Have realistic expectations. Often, people have their feelings hurt because they have unrealistic expectations of the church and, specifically, of the pastor. For instance, Gloria has her feelings hurt because the pastor won't come over and tell her husband that he needs to stop drinking and get a job. Charlie writes the pastor off because the pastor won't come to his workplace and tell his boss that Saturday is the Sabbath and that he should not ask him to work. Old Mrs. Smith doesn't want to come to church anymore because the pastor would not drive her all over town every Tuesday to do her errands.

We can sympathize with each of these people in their predicaments, but the work of the pastor is not to settle domestic disputes, to negotiate work arrangements, or to serve as a taxi driver. Some people just want the pastor to do for them what they should do for themselves. Even if another person's help is needed, it does not always have to be the pastor who ends up doing it. Mrs. Smith's money won't earn any more interest in the bank just because the pastor drove her there. These expectations are unrealistic.

3. Let your leaders be human. Right up there with unrealistic expectations is the tendency to idolize or deify the pastor or other leaders. This leads to nothing but disillusionment. The Wizard of Oz looked pretty impressive until the curtain was drawn aside to reveal nothing but a worn-out magician with a few simple tricks.

Likewise, you may be pretty impressed with your pastor, until you see that he has feet of clay. If your pastor is saying one thing and doing another—playing the part of the hypocrite—then he needs to be confronted. But if he is just doing the best he can and is revealing that he is nothing more than human, give him some space. Allow him to be a mere mortal. The pastor and his family live their lives in a fishbowl open to the inspection of all. So, naturally, you might expect that every now and then he (or a member of his family) might do something that may not live up to your standards. When the pastor's son misbehaves in church, or you see the pastor mowing the lawn in a T-shirt and old jeans on Sunday, don't let it disillusion you.

4. Set a better example. One of the best ways to combat hurt and disappointment is to let it urge you on to doing better in return. You remember the golden rule? Instead of returning hurt for hurt, turn the other cheek. Paul wrote:

If your enemy hungers, feed him; if he thirsts, give him a drink; for in so doing you will heap coals of fire on his head. Do not be overcome by evil, but overcome evil with good (Romans 12:20, 21).

Your bitter experiences can be like stones around your neck that sink you, or they can be stepping stones to hold you up!

JoAnne had her motives misunderstood by a college admissions advisor who was probably having a bad day. When she sincerely asked what classes she should take, he told her, "It doesn't matter; you're probably only here to get married anyway." She was devastated by his comment and left without enrolling.

Several years later, JoAnne ended up working in that same college office. The advisor had long since left for another job, but she always remembered his unthinking, unkind comment and determined that she would not follow his example. She made sure to treat each person kindly, as if his or her motives were the very best, even if they seemed otherwise. JoAnne had the privilege of having several students tell her they had enrolled in that school because she had been so kind and helpful when they were confused and not really sure if they even wanted to be there.

By letting your hurts fuel your determination to live by a higher standard and be a better example, you, too, can have the privilege of being a positive influence for the cause of Christ in your church.

If you have been hurt in church, chances are there are others who have been hurt by the same thing or person. Find out who these hurting people are, not so you can join forces and wage a counterattack but so you can minister to them. Which brings me to the last survival tip.

5. Help the hurting. One of the best ways to heal your own hurts is to realize that others hurt also. Some even more deeply than you do. As we seek to comfort others with the comfort with which we are comforted, the blessing comes back to us.

Surviving Hurt and Dissapointment

Let the burden of your own weakness and sorrow and pain be cast upon the compassionate Saviour. Open your heart to His love, and let it flow out to others. Remember that all have trials hard to bear, temptations hard to resist, and you may do something to lighten these burdens. Express gratitude for the blessings you have; show appreciation of the attentions you receive. Keep the heart full of the precious promises of God, that you may bring forth from this treasure, words that will be a comfort and strength to others. This will surround you with an atmosphere that will be helpful and uplifting.

Let it be your aim to bless those around you, and you will find ways of being helpful, both to the members of your own family and to others (*The Ministry of Healing*, 257, 258).

If you have been hurt, disappointed, or disillusioned, determine to become a source of blessing in your church. Always remember, when passing through these valleys of discouragement, you need to be on your guard, because there are wolves who love to prey upon wounded members.

Keep reading.

Chapter 14

Surviving Critical Ministries

I know this, that after my departure savage wolves will come in among you, not sparing the flock. Also from among yourselves men will rise up, speaking perverse things, to draw away the disciples after themselves (Acts 20:29, 30).

You know a ministry has become too critical when:

> . . . pictures of conference personnel appear in their publications with the words *WANTED* and *REWARD.*

> . . . their sermons deal more with putting people down than lifting Jesus up.

> . . . they believe most church pastors are really Jesuit priests working undercover, specializing in hypnosis.

During the Gulf War of 1991, our country witnessed an interesting development. Out of the one hundred or so U.S. casualties of Desert Storm, most of the deaths were the result of what is called "friendly fire." Friendly fire is when our troops are accidentally fired upon by their own men or allied forces. Imagine that—a war where most of the deaths are not caused by the enemy but by our own side!

Sadly, we are now seeing that same disaster in God's church, where most of the injuries are not caused from persecution from the outside but rather from forces within. The only difference is that the friendly fire in the church is not accidental. The devil knows that he can cause the greatest havoc to the church by planting his representatives within the body.

We have far more to fear from within than from without. The hindrances to strength and success are far greater from the church itself than from the world. . . . But how often have the professed advocates of the truth proved the greatest obstacle to its advancement (*Selected Messages*, 1:122).

We remember that the greatest threat against David was not when he fought Goliath, but rather when he was pursued by his own king, Saul, and his own son, Absalom. Joseph was sold into slavery by his own brothers; Moses fled from Egypt, not because the Egyptians were enslaving his people but rather because his people were fighting among themselves. And, of course, Jesus was crucified by His own people, under the pretense of holiness and love for the law.

In recent years, a number of independent ministries have developed the belief that it is their mission to purify the church by verbally assassinating their brethren. You can get rid of a headache by cutting off your head, but there are better methods.

As we near the end of time and the work of God expands, you will see more and more independent ministries springing up. Some are called by God and offer useful specialized services. These ministries work in cooperation with the denomination to build up the church, but I'm sorry to say that some do not.

As the apostle Paul says: "Test all things; hold fast what is good" (1 Thessalonians 5:21).

You should give an independent ministry the benefit of the doubt until you taste whether it is sweet or sour. However, you don't have to keep drinking once you have found it to be bitter.

On any spring day in North America, you can find two very different birds. One of these birds soars like an eagle and looks perfectly elegant—from a distance. The other bird has the appearance of a common insect, darting around nervously.

If you would take a longer and closer look at these birds, you would find these two birds to be completely opposite from what they first appeared to be.

The bird that soars like an eagle is, in reality, a buzzard, or vulture. He is flying high, not to be closer to heaven, but to have a better view of any poor dead or dying creature. If he sees a bunny or puppy that has been hit by a car, the buzzard will plop down to earth and feast upon the victim.

The other little bird is the hummingbird. It flits from one blossom to another with its iridescent body shimmering in the light, looking for that which is bright, beautiful, and sweet.

We have the same spring day, the same country meadow. Just different birds. One bird is always looking for a dead and decomposing carcass; the other is looking for flowers and nectar. It has been said, "Two men looked out of prison bars; one saw mud, and one saw stars." I've discovered that people generally find what they are looking for!

In the church, we have both buzzards and hummingbirds. Some independent ministries have become like vultures, always focusing on anything scandalous and negative. They search out, dig up, and concentrate on any corruption they can find. They take hearsay and quotes out of context and broadcast their grisly findings everywhere. These ministries prey upon new Christians, members of the church who have been wounded by others, and those who have grown disillusioned by glaring imperfections in God's organized work.

Every religion in this world has elements of truth. This is what makes them appealing. In the same way, some of the critical ministries I know have some truth mixed in with a lot of false or exaggerated information. I will at times agree with some of their observations, but I hasten to add, I do not agree with their focus or most of their conclusions.

Here's what Paul said:

> I urge you, brethren, note those who cause divisions and offenses, contrary to the doctrine which you learned, and avoid them. For those who are such do not serve our Lord Jesus Christ, but their own belly, and by smooth words and flattering speech deceive the hearts of the simple (Romans 16:17, 18).

Perhaps I should define what is a "critical ministry." To begin with, I want to state that not all criticism is bad. The Bible and Spirit of Prophecy are filled with constructive criticism, sometimes called reproof or counsel or warnings from God. When given in love, for the purpose of building up the church and paving the way to the cross, criticism can be healthy. On the other hand, a critical ministry criticizes to tear down what it considers competition while wearing a mask of holy concern.

Criticisms and biblical answers

1. Tithes and offerings. The criticism: "The church leaders are squandering and misdirecting tithes and offerings. The denomination is in a state of worldly compromise. You should no longer send your tithes and offerings to such an organization, because you will be held accountable. Find a ministry preaching the straight, loud trumpet—sigh-and-cry message—(like us, for instance), and send your tithe to them."

The answer: God's church has in its fellowship some who are guilty of almost any sin you can imagine, and probably some you cannot imagine! Though it breaks our heavenly Father's heart, from the time of Adam to the present, the church has always had in its midst hypocrites who have left a greasy, sinful trail in its history. The Bible speaks of adultery, incest, murder, lying, drunkenness, and general depravity, just to begin a list.

In light of this, are we to withhold our tithes and offerings from the church because some people in positions of leadership are squandering or even stealing from the funds? If so, we probably would not have supported Jesus when He walked the earth. He had a thieving Judas in His administration. Did Jesus know that Judas was stealing? Of course, He did! Then, why did our Lord not seek to expose him?

Was the church corrupt at the time of Christ? Yes. Then, what about the time Jesus blessed the widow, who gave her last two cents to support the church? The leaders of that church were about to call for Jesus' blood (Mark 12:43; *The Desire of Ages*, 615). In spite of that, Jesus commended the widow's generosity to the church.

What about the time when Hannah gave her greatest gift, her only son, to God's church? It was also a time of deep spiritual corruption. The priests were completely given to wickedness. Yet God blessed Hannah for her offering (1 Samuel 1:28).

God's command does not read, "Bring your tithes and offerings to the storehouse if the priests are all converted." Regardless of the spiritual condition of some in positions of leadership, we are commanded to give, and we will be blessed (Malachi 3:10)!

If you are disillusioned with church leaders, please don't let those who would tell you not to support the church entice you to sin by deceiving you into rechanneling your support. Please read what Ellen White wrote in regard to this:

Some have been dissatisfied, and have said, "I will no

longer pay my tithe, for I have no confidence in the way things are managed at the heart of the work." But will you rob God because you think the management of the work is not right? Make your complaint, plainly and openly, in the right spirit, to the proper ones. Send in your petitions for things to be adjusted and set in order; but do not withdraw from the work of God, and prove unfaithful, because others are not doing right (*Testimonies for the Church*, 9:249).

The U.S. government squanders billions of dollars every year, and I may protest the waste, but I'm not leaving my country, and I still pay my taxes.

Some people will say, "Doug, I'm not robbing God. I send my tithe to Squeaky Clean Ministry."

Very few critical ministries work to save the lost off the streets. They usually zero in on pulling folks out of the Adventist churches. Your tithe should go "to the storehouse" to help preach the gospel around the world. Most independent ministries are not evangelizing the world. Not to mention that if everyone sent their tithes to independent ministries, there would be no pastors, no evangelists, no missionaries; the work around the world would crumble.

The people who send their tithes and offerings to a critical ministry while still attending a local Seventh-day Adventist church are spiritual sponges. They are looting the church, soaking up all the nice benefits that others have paid for, and they give nothing in return except negative advice.

A critical ministry is funded by appealing to your dissatisfaction with the church. This tends to create a real conflict of interest. If church support goes up, the funding of private ministries goes down, threatening their existence. If they can keep dissatisfaction alive, their offerings increase, ensuring their livelihood.

Therefore, they have a vested interest in fueling your fire by faulting the church.

You can decide for yourself, but I would beware of any

"ministry" that survives and thrives by generating disapproval of the church. The more reasons they can supply to be disappointed with the church, the more money they can make. One only needs to get ten people to send their tithe to produce a large salary just from criticizing.

Hence, people who take the position that we should not support the church financially until it's holy enough will never support the church, because they will never feel it is holy enough. I believe, in some cases, those who withhold their tithe while pointing to problems in the church are doing this as a diversionary tactic to cloak their selfishness or bitter feelings.

2. Christian standards. The criticism: "The church is in a complete state of apostasy. In every area from dress to diet, from music to magazines, the denomination has conformed to the world. The only hope for revival is to spread the literature of our Squeaky Clean Ministry, which still preaches the straight, loud-trumpet, sigh-and-cry testimony."

The answer: Is the church in a state of apostasy? Yes. Complete apostasy? No! There are still thousands of knees that have not bowed to Baal. But it is true, in some places, the church has compromised Bible standards.

If you have ever traveled around the world, you will find that the spiritual condition of the church differs widely from place to place. In countries where Christians are persecuted for their faith, members are more devoted to the Lord and the truth. In North America, with all our abundance, church has become more a social assembly than a place where we gather to satisfy our hunger and thirst for God.

Now, I realize I am generalizing a little, but I've also noticed in the large cities, with all the distractions of rats racing around us in the fast lane, you will find even more worldly compromise. For instance, way back around A.D. 400, Christians in the big city of Rome had the reputation of being the poorest example of Christianity in the empire.

Yet when critical ministries are describing the decay of standards, they scrape the bottom and pull up a sample of the worst North American Adventist city church they can find. They then hold it forth as the example of all Adventists everywhere.

During the Los Angeles riots in the spring of 1992, Karen and I were in Russia conducting evangelistic meetings. The Russian media, always wanting to portray America in the worst possible light, covered the riots by showing video footage of a neighborhood burning, then saying, "People were rioting in all the major cities of the United States." Because of dishonest journalism, the Russian people thought all American cities were in flames in a state of riotous bedlam, when in reality the violence was mostly confined to communities in Los Angeles County.

Many critical ministries have adopted this method of dishonest, or grossly exaggerated, journalism, taking an isolated case of scandal and making it appear universal.

History reveals a cycle of Christian revivals being followed by a slow spiritual decline. Spiritual decline brings withdrawn blessings and God's judgment. God's judgment often brings repentance and revival. I believe God is about to allow severe judgment to fall upon His people in North America. For some, it will bring repentance and reform; for others, hardening of hearts. The critical ministries, however, will never bring a revival.

Another consistent trait I have noticed among these ministries is the apparent lack of balance in their people and publications. To prove a certain point, their articles contain a compilation of quotes from the Spirit of Prophecy or the Bible. These quotes are often taken out of proper context and presented in a concentrated form. This makes an altogether different impression than intended by the writer.

One afternoon, Karen and I went to town to get some needed groceries. Our son Micah stayed home to do some chores. As we were delayed in returning home, he became impatient waiting for dinner. So he prepared his own meal. When we arrived home, Micah was sitting on the couch with glassy eyes and looking a little pale.

"Son, are you OK?" I asked.

"Not really," he moaned.

"Are you hungry?" Karen inquired. He just shook his head.

"Did you eat?" He nodded Yes.

"Well, what did you have to eat?" I pressed.

"A can of vegetarian vegetable soup," he sighed.

Then I asked, "Did you add water to the soup?" Suddenly he turned to me with a look of quizzical surprise.

"You're supposed to add water?"

Micah's stomach was sour from eating a can of concentrated vegetable soup. When mixed with water, soup is good food, but without the proper balance, it will make you sick.

If I were to take everything the Bible says about fasting and repentance and compile those statements together in concentrated form, it would be well calculated to depress you.

Or if I were to compile everything Ellen White says on the subject of Christian perfection and detach it from her statements about God's love and forgiveness, it would also prove discouraging. Not only did John the Baptist preach, "Repent," he also said, "Behold the Lamb of God that takes away the sin of the world" (John 1:29). We must remember to mix Living Water with stinging conviction, love with law, mercy with justice, personal self-control with tolerance for others. We must have balance.

The people who usually march in the ranks of critical ministries do not seem to be a happy group (alas, have I become critical too?).

When participating in a Communion service, a gentleman who was an avid supporter of one of these ministries ran up to me with his face all contorted and said, "Pastor, this is awful!"

"What is?" I asked.

He barked out, "We should not have crosses in our churches!" I looked around curious to find the cross that had so offended my brother.

"Where is it?" I asked.

"It's right on top of the Communion-tray covers."

On top of the Communion table were the metal trays containing the bread and grape juice. On the lid of each tray was a little cross two inches high that served as a handle.

I did not mean to be offensive, but without thinking, I asked the man, "If I believed like you, would I act like you?"

His expression of panic turned to one of solemn reflection, and he walked away.

We become like what we believe. If our beliefs are negative, we become negative; if our religion is out of balance, we become out of balance.

3. Out of Babylon. The criticism: "Because the Adventist organization is so far removed from the faith of our fathers, to remain on the books as a member is an act of treason against God. We recommend you leave the organized work. Have your name dropped from the membership list, and join us, the true, invisible, spiritual church."

The answer: One of the first principles of sales is, "If the customer does not have a need for your product, then create a need." In order for critical ministries to increase their support, they must draw from the organized body. To do this, they must appear to offer a service the denomination cannot supply. That is, the only correct interpretation of certain scriptures, inside information of conference coverups, or unpublished manuscripts, just to name a few of the more common tactics used. Of course, the only alternative to leaving the organized church is to join a disorganized work.

If you want to get someone to jump out of an airplane, first convince him you have a good parachute for him. Then, convince him the plane is going to crash. This is why critical ministries work so frantically to run down the denomination. The supporters of critical ministries are almost never made up of souls saved by those ministries, but rather disgruntled former Seventh-day Adventists.

The following statement is an important one:

> Those who have proclaimed the Seventh-day Adventist Church as Babylon, have made use of the *Testimonies* in giving their position a seeming support; but why is it that they did not present that which for years has been the burden of my message—the unity of the church? Why did they not quote the words of the angel, "Press together, press together, press together"? Why did they not repeat

the admonition and state the principle, that "in union there is strength, in division there is weakness"? It is such messages as these men have borne that divide the church, and put us to shame before the enemies of truth; and in such messages is plainly revealed the specious working of the great deceiver, who would hinder the church from attaining unto perfection in unity. These teachers follow the sparks of their own kindling, move according to their own independent judgment, and cumber the truth with false notions and theories. They refuse the counsel of their brethren, and press on in their own way until they become just what Satan would desire to have them—unbalanced in mind (*Testimonies to Ministers*, 56).

Again, I want to say that spiritual conditions in some parts of the Seventh-day Adventist work are deplorable. But does a low spiritual tide provide biblical reasons for a Christian to jump overboard?

When God's people were killing the prophets and worshiping Baal, and Jezebel was on the throne with Ahab, Elijah thought he had no choice but to leave. When he found himself alone in the desert, God asked, "What are you doing here, Elijah?" God told him if he would see things improve, he needed to stop running away from the problems and get back to His people (1 Kings 17–19).

It's a common practice for the critical ministries to cleverly arrange statements of Ellen White in such a way so as to appear she condoned, even encouraged, leaving this church. There is, however, one glaring inconsistency in their logic. In spite of the fact that the same problems existed in the denomination in her day, i.e., worldliness, lowering of standards, and elements of conference corruption and financial irresponsibility, she remained a tithe-paying, church-attending, name-on-the-books member to her dying day.

She said:

When anyone is drawing apart from the organized

body of God's commandmentkeeping people, when he begins to . . . pronounce judgment against them, then you may know that God is not leading him (*Selected Messages*, 3:18).

Of course, our best example is Jesus. Even after most of His people rejected His teaching, plotted His murder, and crucified Him, even denied His resurrection, the first place that He sent His disciples after the outpouring of the Holy Spirit was back to the same people, the same temple (Acts 3).

You can't clean a house from the outside. Those who leave the church because of worldliness in the church lose their influence to help reform the church. The salt has lost its savor. This is just what the devil wants you to do.

It's like the old fisherman who said, "When in rough water, I found it much easier to bail out my boat while still in it."

When, because of their lack of faith, murmuring, complaining, and lusting after Egypt, the children of Israel had to leave the borders of the Promised Land and were forced to return and wander in the wilderness, they did not go alone! Faithful ones like Moses, Aaron, Joshua, and Caleb did not break off by themselves but stayed with their weaker, faithless brethren. Not only did Moses stay with them, God stayed with them too!

The church of Christ on earth will be imperfect, but God does not destroy His church because of its imperfection (*Testimonies to Ministers*, 46).

I believe the Seventh-day Adventist Church today is modern Israel. It has all the same pitfalls and problems of ancient Israel, but God is still with this movement. Anyone who encourages you to splinter off to be part of a new "holier fellowship" is a wolf in sheep's clothing and an agent of the devil.

You may be wondering, as we near the end of time and our religion is found to be against the law, should we ever leave the visible organization? You guessed it; keep reading.

Chapter 15

When to Leave the Church

Paul said to the centurion and to the soldiers, Except these abide in the ship, ye cannot be saved (Acts 27:31, KJV).

You know it is time to leave the church when:

> . . . they set up a stake in the church courtyard for burning heretics.

> . . . they try to tattoo "666" on your forehead.

> . . . they have a Friday-night dance contest in the sanctuary.

Two teenage brothers, Bo and Joe, decided to take advantage of the warm weather one Sunday afternoon and drove down to the ocean pier to go swimming.

"I can't wait to dive in," Bo said.

"Me either," Joe answered as they parked the car.

They changed into their swim trunks and headed toward the pier. It stood high above a rocky shoreline and led out into the water where the waves crashed on the pilings below.

"Last one in is a rotten egg," yelled Bo as he ran down the pier and dove off the end.

"Hey, wait for me," Joe answered as he ran to the end of the pier. Being a little more cautious than his brother, Joe paused to look over the end of the pier before diving off. There, to his horror, the body of his brother lay floating in the surf, his neck

broken by the rocks that lay just below the surface of the water. A young teenager lost his life by diving at low tide while the waves were out. He didn't know when to jump.

You may think Bo was not very smart not to stop to look before he dove, but many Christians today are diving out of the church like lemmings running blindly off a cliff into the sea. They never stop to look before they leap—to think about whether or not there are rocks below. They just see a problem in the church and follow those who say, "Last one out is a rotten egg."

It is easy to get discouraged when you consider all the potential problems one may encounter in a church. There are so many voices out there, constantly reminding us of all the hypocrisy and failures in the church. Some independent ministries are ever providing tabloid information—regurgitating present and past scandals, the squandering of money, lack of the Holy Spirit, the famine of real Bible preaching, etc.—as reasons to leave the church.

You may wonder, What's the use of pretending I am the Titanic captain, and I'm going down with the ship? Can't I be part of God's church without being part of a denomination or the organization? Must I endure pathetic preaching and spiritless fellowship from one week to the next? Is there a time to leave the church?

Yes, there is a time to leave the church!

When the church doctrines are no longer the teachings of Christ, when you are no longer allowed to preach and practice the truth within its fellowship, then obviously you have no choice but to go somewhere else.

But my question to you is—When that happens, will there be anywhere else to go?

There is a story in the Bible about a terrible storm at sea in which Paul and his shipmates nearly perished (Acts 27). For fourteen long days, that little ship, burdened with 276 souls, was lashed by the merciless, cold, dark sea. As the boat pitched and rolled, the passengers began to throw everything overboard (including their lunch). They were probably seasick and had given up all hope that they would survive. The last place in the world they wanted to be was on that boat, but nobody jumped overboard.

In the same way, you may think, God's ship—the church, with all its problems—is the last place you want to be, but I promise you this, you are much better off being tossed about in the church than being in the water with the sharks.

Reading on, the Bible tells us that as Paul and his shipmates neared land, some of the sailors wanted to get off the ship while pretending to help:

> Some of the sailors planned to abandon the ship, and lowered the emergency boat as though they were going to put out anchors from the prow (Acts 27:30, TLB).

In other words, they were saying, "We're going to take a lifeboat and sneak off by ourselves, and we'll leave the others on the ship."

Some people are doing this in the church now. They are branching off by themselves. Paul told the guard in charge:

"Unless these men stay in the ship, you cannot be saved" (Acts 27:31).

Did the soldiers say, "Every man for himself," and join the offshoots by heading for a lifeboat? No. Scripture records, "Then the soldiers cut away the ropes of the skiff, and let it fall off" (Acts 27:32).

The lifeboat was cut away to drop off empty into the sea in order to keep the crew together.

Why is this story in the Bible? For our encouragement and instruction. Paul is saying that unless we stick together, we're not going to make it to the kingdom. And I believe as we, God's people, near shore (the end of time), God is reminding us that we must stay together in spite of the storm. I think He also wants us to cut the ropes to the lifeboats and make a commitment to stay with the ship.

When someone encourages you to be an escape artist, tell them, "Why should I leave? God has promised to bring me safely to shore if I stay with His ship." They may answer that there are too many sinners in the ship, that it can't possibly be God's vessel. But, in our Bible story, Paul tells us the ship was loaded down with prisoners and criminals on their way to judgment. But the message was that they needed to stay together.

Eventually, they did have to leave the ship, but only when it could no longer hold them and it had busted to smithereens on the rocks. At that point, they had to grab what was left of the ship—just the pieces—and make it to shore.

This is how God's church is going to be in the last days. I believe it will become illegal for our church to operate as a visible organization. Our church, the ship, will break apart as we near the shore of the end of time. Then, we're just going to have to make our own way to shore, clinging to parts of the old ship. We'll have to gather in small companies to strengthen and encourage one another.

Acts 27:24 gives one of the reasons why God will preserve us in His church. It reads:

"Do not be afraid, Paul; you must be brought before

When to Leave the Church

Caesar: and indeed God has granted you all those who sail with you."

In case you missed it, God is promising Paul that his life will be spared so that he can be a witness to Caesar. In the same way, near the end of time, each one of us who remains faithful may be called to be a witness to the worldly powers that be. God wants us to bring the last message of hope to a dying world. If we jump ship, we'll miss that opportunity. We are doomed to drown if we try to cross a stormy ocean with nothing but a rubber duck and a bathing suit.

When the wave that breaks the ship apart finally hits, grab onto anything that floats, and swim for shore. I don't know what form that wave will take—government decrees or religious persecution—or when it will come. But I do know things are going to get a lot worse, so we need to be prepared.

The way to be ready is to be daily in prayer and Bible study and in putting on the robe of Christ's righteousness. When storms threaten and those last waves hit, that robe will be our life jacket.

That's the way it is with our church. Some people feel as though it is the church that will safely bring them to the shores of eternal life. These people are only along for the ride and lose their faith in the time of storm. Others have placed their faith in Christ's life, death, and ministry and live in obedience to Him. They are daily placing their faith in Him through prayer, study, and service. They are also in His church but know that when the waves hit, He will be the One to hold them up, not the church. So long as the ship is afloat, they are on board, not as tourists, but as crew members. Not until the ship sinks do they try to make it to shore by any other means.

Friends, that's the kind of person I want to be, the one wearing the life jacket of Christ's righteousness. After all, that's the only way to survive and succeed.

Chapter 16

Not Just Surviving–Succeeding!

The thief cometh not, but for to steal, and to kill, and to destroy: I am come that they might have life, and that they might have it more abundantly (John 10:10, KJV).

You know you are succeeding when:

> . . . you are so close to God that the devil knows your name.

> . . . you are not just a hearer of the word, but a doer.

> . . . your children rise up and call you blessed.

> . . . the conference president asks you to autograph his Bible.

A few years back, my brother, Falcon, started a summer camp in the Florida Keys for children with cystic fibrosis. From time to time, I would attend camp to help as a counselor-pastor. Because our father was in the airline business, he would sometimes donate one of the life rafts, stored on passenger jets for emergencies. The children loved to play on these rafts.

I remember the first time we went down to the beach with the kids dragging one of these large yellow rafts in its folded condition. When we pulled the red cord, all the children stepped back and watched with wide-eyed amazement. The raft exploded into shape, automatically using pressurized air. After a few wonder-filled moments, we stood before a large yellow circular raft designed to sustain the lives of twenty people for several weeks on the open sea.

We pushed the vessel into the shallow water, and the campers played with it until they were all exhausted. When the kids were through, I pulled the raft back to the shore to look it over.

I noticed a large lump with a zipper over it in the middle of the raft. Opening the pouch, I discovered it was filled with all kinds of tightly packed survival gear. One by one, I pulled the objects out and examined them. There was a water-distilling kit for turning saltwater into fresh water, a fishing kit, a first-aid kit, a raft-patching kit, flares, vitamins, a special light that comes on when the battery is placed in saltwater, shark repellent, and sunscreen lotion. Everything needed to support life, provide a degree of comfort, and promote rescue was there.

Then my heart skipped a beat when I reached into the survival pouch and pulled out a Bible! At first, I thought there must be a Christian who works at the factory where they stock these rafts who decided to stick in this Bible.

But I later learned that all the rafts were supplied with Bibles. Evidently, the company that designed the rafts conducted interviews with a number of people who had been lost at sea in rafts to find out what they needed most. Among all the articles mentioned, many said they needed a Bible to strengthen their faith and renew their hope. As World War II captain Eddie Rickenbacker, who, with his men, drifted in a raft at sea for about a month, said, "It was the little Bible we had that saved us."

Whether you are the pilot of an airplane, the captain of a ship, or just a crew member, it is essential to know where to find the survival gear and to make sure it is well stocked.

Likewise, all church members need a survival kit on their journey to the Promised Land, as they can count on a few "eternal life"–threatening situations along the way.

This special section is added just to make sure you know what you'll need—not only to survive in church but to succeed in your Christian walk.

Survival gear with spiritual application

1. Food (the Bible). One must have food to live. We can daily feed on the Word of God and be satisfied by living in obedience to our heavenly Father.

> Jesus said unto them, I am the bread of life. He who comes to Me shall never hunger, and he who believes in Me shall never thirst (John 6:35).

> He answered and said, "It is written, 'Man shall not live by bread alone, but by every word that proceeds from the mouth of God'" (Matthew 4:4).

The abundant life starts by planting the Word of God in your mind every day. Morning is the best time to start, before you face the heat of the day and the cares of life make the manna melt. Don't wait till nighttime. Sometimes we give God a lame offering when we read our Bible all blurry-eyed at the end of the day, before dropping off to sleep. Our brains are operating at a minimum, and often the next morning, we don't even remember what we read.

Martin Luther said we should study the Bible something like the way a person picks apples. First, you shake the whole tree. That would be reading the whole Bible and getting the basic picture. Then you shake the different branches. That would be studying individual books or subjects. And then you shake the twigs and look behind the leaves, digging into each and every verse and word individually.

> When assailed by temptation, look not to circumstances or to the weakness of self, but to the power of the word. All its strength is yours (*The Desire of Ages*, 123).

2. Flashlight. The Word of inspiration is also the flashlight that will help us find our way in the dark. Both the Bible and the Spirit of Prophecy can help us to get back on track.

> Your word is a lamp to my feet and a light to my path (Psalm 119:105).

Then Jesus spoke to them again, saying, "I am the light of the world. He who follows Me shall not walk in darkness, but have the light of life" (John 8:12).

3. Water. Good, pure drinking water is an essential element for survival. It represents our constant need of Jesus Himself, through the Holy Spirit.

Jesus answered and said to her, "Whoever drinks of this water will thirst again, but whoever drinks of the water that I shall give him will never thirst. But the water that I shall give him will become in him a fountain of water springing up into everlasting life" (John 4:13, 14).

On the last day, that great day of the feast, Jesus stood and cried out, saying, "If anyone thirsts, let him come to Me and drink" (John 7:37).

4. Oxygen mask. Prayer is the oxygen mask that can help us breathe the atmosphere of heaven when there is a crisis. Trials or temptations can be like a sudden loss of air pressure that leaves us gasping. Trials are best handled with prayer.

Although there may be a tainted, corrupted atmosphere around us, we need not breathe its miasma, but may live in the pure air of heaven. We may close every door to impure imaginings and unholy thoughts by lifting the soul into the presence of God through sincere prayer. Those whose hearts are open to receive the support and blessing of God will walk in a holier atmosphere than that of earth and will have constant communion with heaven. . . .

Let the soul be drawn out and upward, that God may grant us a breath of the heavenly atmosphere. We may keep so near to God that in every unexpected trial our thoughts will turn to Him as naturally as the flower turns to the sun (*Steps to Christ*, 99, 100).

Your Christian experience cannot grow without prayer. Have

regular times for prayer. The Bible tells us how Daniel had an extraordinary relationship with the Lord. It is definitely connected with his extraordinary devotional life. He prayed three times a day, even when it meant he would lose his life (Daniel 6; Psalm 55:17).

Make sure you don't get in the rut of reciting the same prayers over and over without knowing what you're saying. One night, when having bedtime worship with our children, the youngest prayed, "Dear Jesus, thank You for this food. Please bless it to nourish our bodies. Amen."

The sad thing is, no one else in the family except me noticed he had prayed the dinner prayer instead of the bedtime prayer. So, keep your prayer fresh, from the heart, or it will become a "vain repetition."

Make a list of people and things to pray about; then write down the answers as they come. If you have trouble remembering to start the day with prayer, throw your shoes under the bed before you go to sleep at night, and then when you kneel down in the morning to find them, you might remember to pray!

5. Matches. The Holy Spirit will light us up with love and enthusiasm.

> John answered, saying to them all, "I indeed baptize you with water; but One mightier than I is coming, whose sandal strap I am not worthy to loose. He will baptize you with the Holy Spirit and with fire" (Luke 3:16).

> "The Helper, the Holy Spirit, whom the Father will send in My name, He will teach you all things, and bring to your remembrance all things that I said to you" (John 14:26).

What a loving God He is, to give us the Holy Spirit to light our way.

6. Lotion. To bring comfort from the burning sun and to keep us from drying out spiritually, God has promised to give us the Holy Spirit. "I will pray the Father, and he shall give you another Comforter, that he may abide with you for ever" (John 14:16, KJV).

7. Fishing tackle. Fishing for souls, by sharing your faith, will give you something good to do and something satisfying to feed on. "He said to them, 'Follow me, and I will make you fishers of men'" (Matthew 4:19).

> Jesus came and spake unto them, saying, All power is given unto me in heaven and in earth. Go ye therefore, and teach all nations, baptizing them in the name of the Father, and of the Son, and of the Holy Ghost: teaching them to observe all things whatsoever I have commanded you: and, lo, I am with you alway, even unto the end of the world. Amen (Matthew 28:18-20).

A daily conversion experience through prayer and Bible study and the indwelling of the Holy Spirit will yield a life so full you will want to share it. Just remember, we don't save the world by becoming like the world; you can catch fish without getting in the water. Otherwise you might end up like Jonah—the fish will catch you!

The main reason God gives us the Holy Spirit is to witness.

> "You shall receive power when the Holy Spirit has come upon you; and you shall be witnesses to Me in Jerusalem, and in all Judaea and Samaria, and to the end of the earth" (Acts 1:8).

Every Christian is called to share his faith, to exercise it like a muscle. As you use it, it gets stronger. If you don't use it, it will atrophy and wither away.

> Remember that the exercise of faith is the one means of preserving it. Should you sit always in one position, without moving, your muscles would become strengthless and your limbs would lose the power of motion. The same is true in regard to your religious experience. You must have faith in the promises of God. . . . Faith will perfect itself

in exercise and activity (*In Heavenly Places*, 104).

You may not be a preacher or know how to give a Bible study—but every child of God has some talents or tools that God has given to be used in His service. Just read through the list and you'll see that these fruits are just meant for sharing.

> The fruit of the Spirit is love, joy, peace, longsuffering, gentleness, goodness, faith, meekness, temperance: against such there is no law (Galatians 5:22, 23, KJV).

When a church reaches out to others, when it begins to minister to the needs of individuals as Jesus did, its actions will smother and choke our selfish natures.

8. Life jacket. The robe of Christ's righteousness is the only life jacket that will keep a sinner afloat even when the church itself seems to be shipwrecked.

> These are they which came out of great tribulation, and have washed their robes, and made them white in the blood of the Lamb (Revelation 7:14).

The bottom line

After covering such a wide variety of problems that a person might encounter in the church, it's important to bring things back into perspective. Our church experience is not something to be endured, but to be enjoyed. Our hope is not simply to survive, but to succeed. It should be a sweet, fulfilling experience.

Let's remind ourselves of the three basic reasons why we have trouble just surviving in church.

First, most of the conflicts that we encounter in the church family are multiplied a thousand times over if we are not fully surrendered to Jesus or converted. Selfishness is almost always at the heart of our failures, while love will be the secret of our success. Before the crucifixion of Jesus, the disciples were bickering and arguing among themselves as to which of them was the greatest. They were all being selfish. But after seeing

Jesus die and rise from the grave, a new harmony, humility, and patient tolerance came into their relationships.

That's the main solution right there in a nutshell! We must collide with the cross every day. Jesus said, "If I am lifted up . . . , [I] will draw all peoples to Myself" (John 12:32).

It stands to reason that if we are all drawing closer to Jesus, we will be coming closer to one another. If we remember that we are all big sinners in need of a big Saviour, then we will not be so easily bothered by the petty offenses others.

Second, remember that we must keep our priorities in focus. We are at war with the forces of evil, and Satan's strategy is to create conflict within the Christian camp. We easily fall for the devil's divisive and distracting tactics by becoming so preoccupied with examining our own spiritual belly buttons while the world perishes in sin around us. We too frequently major on the minors and minor with the majors.

Third, remember that we will each have to answer for ourselves. "Every one of us shall give account of himself to God" (Romans 14:12).

The church is not responsible for your salvation—*you are*. The pastor is not responsible for your relationship with Jesus—*you are*. Nobody will stand before the Lord in the judgment day and successfully blame her lost condition on the pastor or parents or a cantankerous group of church members!

Do you need the Holy Spirit? Then ask. "If you then, being evil, know how to give good gifts to your children, how much more will your heavenly Father give the Holy Spirit to those who ask Him!" (Luke 11:13).

Do you need wisdom? The Bible says to ask God.

> If any of you lack wisdom, let him ask of God, that giveth to all men liberally, and upbraideth not; and it shall be given him (James 1:5, KJV).

Would you like to see a revival in your church? Then ask your heavenly Father to revive you. And in so doing, your church will begin reviving.

Conclusion

***Commit your way to the Lord, trust also in Him,
and He shall bring it to pass (Psalm 37:5).***

When a bride and groom stand before the minister, they make some very broad and permanent vows. Promises that are meant to last forever. What gives them the confidence that they can fulfill these vows? They have a strong love and a deep sense of commitment.

In like manner, when we join God's church family and make our baptismal vows, we should understand that this means "in sickness and health, in prosperity and adversity, in the sunshine and the rain." God's church family will have many of the same highs and lows of any earthly family. But if we love Jesus and commit ourselves to love His people, it becomes a precious experience that will survive any trial.

I think we sometimes underestimate how much God can do through one completely converted, committed Christian! Through the prayers and faith of one ordinary man, Elijah, the nation of Israel was turned back to God. The Bible promise is:

The effective, fervent prayer of a righteous man avails much. Elijah was a man with a nature like ours, and he prayed earnestly that it would not rain; and it did not rain on the land for three years and six months. And he prayed again, and the heaven gave rain, and the earth produced its fruit (James 5:16-18).

And, of course, the example of complete commitment is Jesus.

Who, when He was reviled, did not revile in return; when He suffered, He did not threaten, but committed Himself to Him who judges righteously (1 Peter 2:23).

King David reminds us: "Commit your way to the Lord, trust also in Him, and He shall bring it to pass" (Psalm 37:5).

Paul said: "I know whom I have believed, and am persuaded that He is able to keep what I have committed to Him until that day" (2 Timothy 1:12).

Here is one of my favorite statements from the writings of Ellen White:

The greatest want of the world is the want of men—men who will not be bought or sold; men who in their inmost souls are true and honest, men who do not fear to call sin by its right name, men whose conscience is as true to duty as the needle to the pole, men who will stand for the right though the heavens fall (*Education*, 57).

Dear friend, I've learned that with God's help, a person can do almost anything, if he really wants to. I have also learned that where there is faith and hope, all things are possible to him who believes. If you truly desire and believe, you can survive and succeed in this church as a vibrant, Spirit-filled Christian.

Without Jesus, we will surely sink in the stormy times ahead.

In the year 1912, as that famous ocean liner, the *Titanic*, was preparing for its maiden voyage, the newspapers were interviewing the captain, John Smith. Because the vessel was designed with sixteen watertight compartments, Captain Smith was heard saying, "God Himself could not sink this ship!" The ship's designers were so confident of its safety that they only equipped the Titanic with a token number of lifeboats.

Then, four days into the maiden voyage, the ship struck an iceberg, the hull ripped open with a three-hundred-foot gash, and within two hours it sank in the dark, icy waters of the North Atlantic.

The *Titanic* was built in Belfast, Ireland, and sixteen of the skilled mechanics who helped build her had been invited on the maiden voyage. When the tragic news reached Belfast that the unsinkable ship had gone down on the very first journey, and further, that all sixteen of these men had perished, the town was paralyzed with grief. Strong men would meet on the street, embrace, cry, and part without a word.

That first Sunday after the disaster, an American preacher was invited to speak at the large church where all sixteen of these deceased men had attended. As the minister stepped to the platform, the congregation was filled with dignitaries from all over the British Empire. And before him were many newly made widows and orphans. Sobbing could be heard on every side.

The American pastor chose as his sermon title "The Unsinkable Ship." When I first read this, I thought, "That was poor taste to remind the people of the folly of their bragging." But he was not referring to that eleven-story vessel, longer than a football field, that went down in 13,000 feet of cold water, taking with it 1,500 lives. Instead, the preacher was speaking of a small old fishing boat on a dark inland sea, lashed by the wind, beaten by the waves, swamped with water. Yet that little vessel was unsinkable because Jesus was in the boat.

Friend, this is the only way to survive in church, and in life—to have Jesus in your boat. Let Him take the ropes and rudder, and He will lead you through the storms of life and safely bring you to heaven's harbor. Make a firm commitment today; ask Him to be your Captain, Lord, and Saviour, to fill you with His Spirit. Then faithfully follow Him wherever He leads.

Why not join me now in making this pledge to Jesus by choosing to put your hand to the plow, holding tight, and never looking back.

> Ruth said: Entreat me not to leave you, or to turn back from following after you; for wherever you go, I will go; and wherever you lodge, I will lodge; your people shall be my people, and your God, my God. Where you die, I will die, and there will I be buried. The Lord do so to me, and more also, if anything but death parts you and me (Ruth 1:16, 17).